改訂版

書いて覚える

文部科学省後援

英検® 3級 合格ノート

松本恵美子

Matsumoto Emiko

高橋書店

はじめに

みなさん，こんにちは。
著者の松本恵美子です。
普段は大学で英語の先生をしています。

みなさんは英語の勉強をするのは得意ですか？
今私が教えている優秀な大学生たちの多くは，中学，高校で英語の勉強を頑張っていました。
彼らと話をしていると「授業で先生が言っている内容はわかったけれども，その予習，復習のために自分ひとりで勉強をするのは苦手だった」という声をよくききます。
英語の勉強に近道はありません。でも，それぞれが好きだと思えるテキストを使ったり，好きな文房具をそろえたり，自分に合った勉強方法にすることで，勉強が長続きしやすくなります。

本書は，英検合格を目指す人たちのニーズのうち，「ひとりでも勉強したい」，「好きなテキストを見つけたい」というリクエストに応えた教材です。みなさんのお悩みを解決すべく，取り組みやすい形式にしています。
楽しく勉強したいみなさんのための，楽しいイラスト付きの使いやすいノート，それが本書『英検合格ノート』です。

お気に入りの場所に座って，お気に入りのシャープペンを持って，最初のページを解いてみてください。ほら，スラスラと書き込めるでしょう。
ページをサクサクめくっていく間に，自然に実力がつくようになっています。

本書を使って，英語がもっと好きになってもらえることを祈っています。

松本恵美子

CONTENTS

＊解答解説は, 別冊にあります。

長文

英作文

リスニング

模擬試験

二次試験(面接)

編集協力 株式会社カルチャー・プロ(中村淳一/佐々木淳)
イラスト ナカニシヒカル
ブックデザイン 喜來詩織(エントツ)
DTP 株式会社シーアンドシー
校正 株式会社鴎来堂
録音 ユニバ合同会社
ナレーター ドミニク・アレン/アン・スレーター/芦澤亜希子

本書の使い方

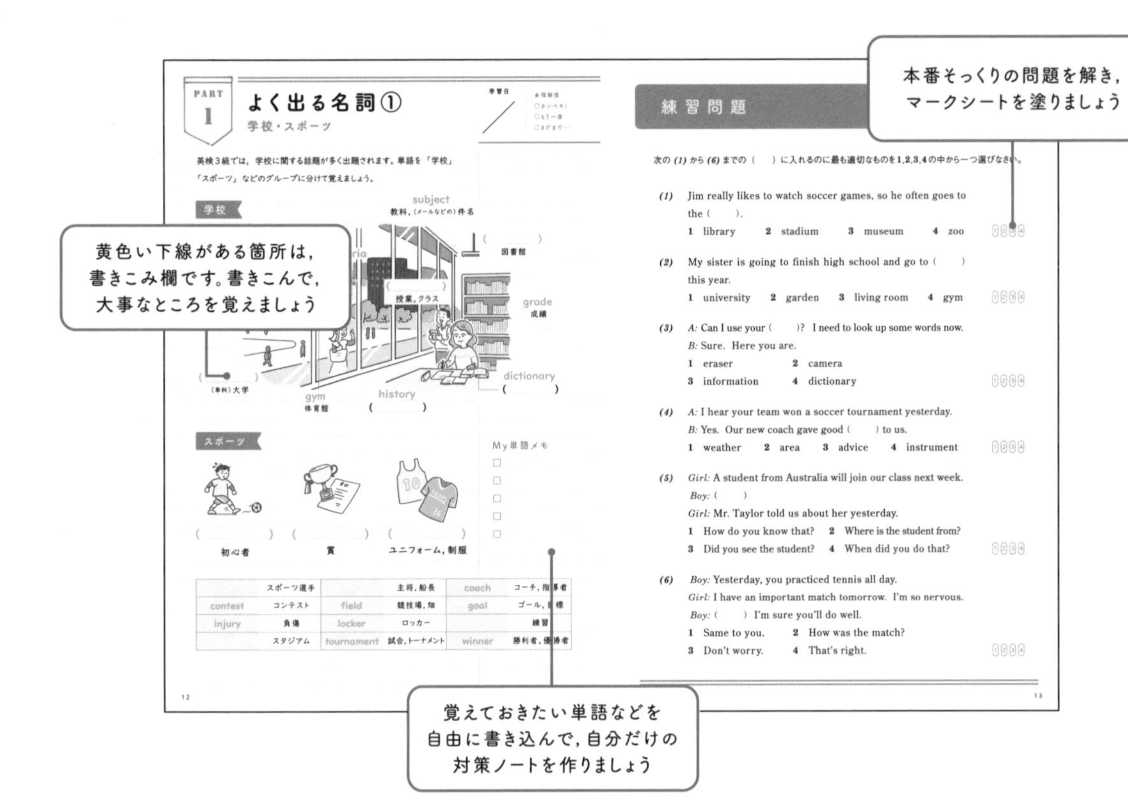
PART 1 よく出る名詞①
学校・スポーツ

学習日

★理解度
□カンペキ!
□もう一度
□まだまだ…

英検3級では，学校に関する話題が多く出題されます。単語を「学校」「スポーツ」などのグループに分けて覚えましょう。

学校

subject
教科，(メールなどの)件名

(　　　) 図書館

(　　　) 授業，クラス

grade 成績

(　　　) (単科)大学

gym 体育館

history (　　　)

dictionary (　　　)

スポーツ

(　　　) 初心者　(　　　) 賞　(　　　) ユニフォーム，制服

My単語メモ
□
□
□
□
□

	スポーツ選手		主将，船長	coach	コーチ，指導者
contest	コンテスト	field	競技場，畑	goal	ゴール，目標
injury	負傷	locker	ロッカー		練習
	スタジアム	tournament	試合，トーナメント	winner	勝利者，優勝者

12

練習問題

次の (1) から (6) までの (　) に入れるのに最も適切なものを1,2,3,4の中から一つ選びなさい。

(1) Jim really likes to watch soccer games, so he often goes to the (　　).
1 library　2 stadium　3 museum　4 zoo

(2) My sister is going to finish high school and go to (　　) this year.
1 university　2 garden　3 living room　4 gym

(3) A: Can I use your (　　)? I need to look up some words now.
B: Sure. Here you are.
1 eraser　2 camera
3 information　4 dictionary

(4) A: I hear your team won a soccer tournament yesterday.
B: Yes. Our new coach gave good (　　) to us.
1 weather　2 area　3 advice　4 instrument

(5) Girl: A student from Australia will join our class next week.
Boy: (　　)
Girl: Mr. Taylor told us about her yesterday.
1 How do you know that?　2 Where is the student from?
3 Did you see the student?　4 When did you do that?

(6) Boy: Yesterday, you practiced tennis all day.
Girl: I have an important match tomorrow. I'm so nervous.
Boy: (　　) I'm sure you'll do well.
1 Same to you.　2 How was the match?
3 Don't worry.　4 That's right.

13

① 答え合わせ

答え合わせはとても重要です。苦手を発見し，間違えた箇所は解きなおしましょう。

解答解説は別冊になっています。別冊は軽くのり付けされているので，そっと手前に引き抜くと取り外せます。

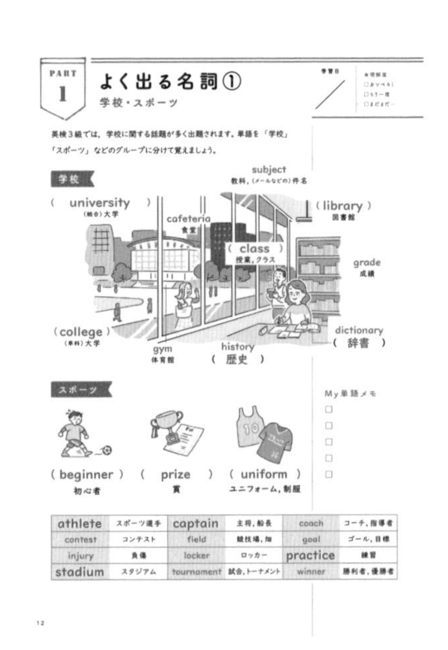
PART 1 よく出る名詞①
学校・スポーツ

学習日

★理解度
□カンペキ!
□もう一度
□まだまだ…

英検3級では，学校に関する話題が多く出題されます。単語を「学校」「スポーツ」などのグループに分けて覚えましょう。

学校

subject
教科，(メールなどの)件名

(university) (総合)大学

(library) 図書館

cafeteria 食堂

(class) 授業，クラス

grade 成績

(college) (単科)大学

gym 体育館

history (歴史)

dictionary (辞書)

スポーツ

(beginner) 初心者　(prize) 賞　(uniform) ユニフォーム，制服

My単語メモ
□
□
□
□
□

athlete	スポーツ選手	captain	主将，船長	coach	コーチ，指導者
contest	コンテスト	field	競技場，畑	goal	ゴール，目標
injury	負傷	locker	ロッカー	practice	練習
stadium	スタジアム	tournament	試合，トーナメント	winner	勝利者，優勝者

12

パッと見て答えがわかるので，答え合わせがラクラク

② 音声

上のマークがあるところは，
音声が収録されています。
音声を聞いて，リスニングと
二次試験（面接）をリアルに
練習しましょう。

音声について

下の二次元コードを読み取るか、URLの専用サイトにアクセスしてください。

［ダウンロードの手順］
①お使いの書籍を選択。
②パスワード入力欄に「27627」と入力する。
③「全音声をダウンロードする」をクリックする。

https://www.takahashishoten.co.jp/audio-dl/eiken/

※音声データは圧縮されたMP3形式です。再生にはファイル解凍ソフトと音声再生ソフトが必要です。
お客様のご利用端末の環境により音声のダウンロード・再生ができない場合は，当社は責任を負いかねます。
ご理解，ご了承いただきますよう，お願いいたします。
※パソコン・スマホ等の操作に関するご質問にはお答えできません。

③ 模擬試験

最後の総仕上げに，模擬試験を解きましょう。
模擬試験は，英検本番の形式と同じですから，記載されている制限時間を守って，本番のつもりで解きましょう。

解答用紙は，別冊の最後のページにあります。切り離して使ってください。

模擬試験

答えは別冊P32～43

本番と同じ形式の模擬試験です。
本番の練習になるように，次の3つを守って解きましょう。
① 筆記試験（96～105ページ）は，65分で解く。
② リスニングテスト（106～109ページ）は，音声を止めないで解く。
③ 筆記試験からリスニングテストまで通して解く。
※解答用紙は別冊の最後のページにあります。

1 次の *(1)* から *(15)* までの（　　）に入れるのに最も適切なものを1, 2, 3, 4の中から一つ選び，その番号のマーク欄をぬりつぶしなさい。

(1) These two bags look the same. What's the (　　) between them?
1 tournament　2 difference　3 action　4 promise

(2) We don't have to run, Steve. We have (　　) time to catch the next bus.
1 quick　2 hot　3 enough　4 clear

(3) *A:* Henry, can you pass me the (　　) on the table? I need them to open this box.
B: OK. Here you are.
1 staplers　2 stores　3 scissors　4 shoes

(4) *A:* Excuse me. I'm looking for toys for my daughter.
B: You can find them on the fourth (　　), sir.
1 floor　2 lesson　3 introduction　4 schedule

(5) *A:* What are you reading, Fred?
B: It's a new (　　) by my favorite writer. I got it yesterday.
1 bicycle　2 suitcase　3 language　4 novel

(6) *A:* Is Ted in the hospital? What (　　)?
B: He was hit by a car this morning.
1 changed　2 happened　3 explained　4 baked

96

受験ガイド

初めての「英検」でも安心して受験できるように，
受験の前に知っておきたいことをまとめました。

特徴・メリット

文部科学省が後援

実用英語の力を育てる7つの級を設定。
学習進度やレベルに応じた
学習目標として最適です。

スピーキング測定

スピーキングを含む4技能を測定。
「使える英語」であなたの
コミュニケーションを広げます。

入試優遇・単位認定

「英検」取得者は
多くの高校・大学の入学試験や
単位認定で優遇されています。

「英検」で海外留学

「英検」は，世界各国の教育機関で海外留学時
の語学力証明資格に認定されています。
「英検」資格で，世界へ羽ばたく道が広がります。

3級の出題レベル・試験内容

3級の出題レベルの目安は「中学卒業程度」とされています。
3級には，一次試験と二次試験があります。一次試験は筆記とリスニング，
二次試験は面接です。一次試験に合格すると，二次試験が受験できます。

〈一次試験の内容〉

		形式	問題数
筆記（65分）	大問1	短文の語句空所補充	15
	大問2	会話文の文空所補充	5
	大問3	長文の内容一致選択	10
	大問4,5	ライティング（Eメール，英作文）	2
リスニング（約25分）	第1部	会話の応答文選択	10
	第2部	会話の内容一致選択	10
	第3部	文の内容一致選択	10

※大問4，5 ライティングは記述式，その他の問題は選択肢から答えを選ぶマークシート方式です。

受験日・受験地

すべての級で，年3回試験が実施されます。第1回は（一次試験 6月／二次試験 7月），
第2回は（一次試験 10月／二次試験 11月），第3回は（一次試験 1月／二次試験 2月）です。
申し込みの締め切りは，一次試験のおよそ1か月前です。全国で試験が実施されているので，
多くの場合，自宅の近くの会場や自分の通う学校で受験できます。

申し込み方法

申し込みには，団体申し込みと個人申し込みの2通りの方法があります。

団体申し込みの場合

学生の場合は，自分が通っている学校で団体申し込みをする場合が多いので，
まずは学校の先生に聞いてみましょう。団体申し込みの場合は，
先生からもらった願書に記入し，先生を通じて願書と検定料を送ります。

個人申し込みの場合

次の3つの方法で，だれでも申し込めます。

- **インターネット申し込み**

「英検」のウェブサイト（https://www.eiken.or.jp/eiken/）から申し込む。

- **コンビニ申し込み**

ローソン，ミニストップ，セブン－イレブン，ファミリーマートなどに
設置されている情報端末機から申し込む。

- **特約書店申し込み**

願書付「英検」パンフレットを無料配布している特約書店で申し込む。

受験や申し込みに関するお問い合わせは，公益財団法人 日本英語検定協会まで
- 「英検」協会公式ウェブサイト https://www.eiken.or.jp/eiken/
- 「英検」サービスセンター TEL 03-3266-8311（個人受付）

一次試験当日の持ち物／チェック・リスト

- □ **一次受験票** ――写真（タテ3cm×ヨコ2.4cm）を必ず貼りつけること
- □ **身分証明書** ――学生証・運転免許証・健康保険証（コピー可）・パスポートなど
- □ **HBの黒鉛筆2・3本，またはシャープペンシル** ――マークしやすいものを選ぼう
- □ **消しゴム**
- □ **腕時計** ――スマートフォン，スマートウォッチ，タイマーつきの時計は，試験中は使えません。アラームなどの音の出る設定は必ず解除しておこう
- □ **スリッパ** ――会場によっては必要なので，受験票に書いてあれば持っていこう

出題形式

ここで，3級の出題内容を確認しておきましょう。
※試験内容等は変わる場合があります。

筆記　65分，32問

大問1

短文の語句空所補充〈15問〉

短い文や，会話文の中の（　　）に適する語句を4つの選択肢の中から選びます。

次の (1) から (15) までの（　　）に入れるのに最も適切なものを1, 2, 3, 4の中から一つ選び，その番号のマーク欄をぬりつぶしなさい。

(1) These two bags look the same. What's the (　　) between them?
1 tournament　2 difference　3 action　4 promise

(2) We don't have to run, Steve. We have (　　) time to catch the next bus.
1 quick　2 hot　3 enough　4 clear

(3) *A:* Henry, can you pass me the (　　) on the table? I need them to open this box.
B: OK. Here you are.

大問2

会話文の文空所補充〈5問〉

会話文の中の（　　）に適する文または文の一部を，4つの選択肢の中から選ぶ問題です。

次の (16) から (20) までの会話について，（　　）に入れるのに最も適切なものを1, 2, 3, 4の中から一つ選び，その番号のマーク欄をぬりつぶしなさい。

(16) *Mother:* Why is your sister crying?
Son: She was running on the way home, and (　　)
1 it's sunny today.　2 that's her bag.
3 she'll be glad.　4 she fell down.

(17) *Granddaughter:* Can I have some cookies, Grandma?
Grandmother: Of course, Sally. (　　)
1 Help yourself.　2 You're right.
3 Try your best.　4 I don't think so.

大問3

長文の内容一致選択〈10問〉

長文は，Ⓐ掲示・案内，ⒷEメール，Ⓒ説明文の3題が出題されます。長文の内容に関する質問の答えとして，もっとも正しいものを選択肢から選ぶ問題です。

次の掲示の内容に関して，(21) と (22) の質問に対する答えとして最も適切なもの，または文を完成させるのに最も適切なものを1, 2, 3, 4の中から一つ選び，その番号のマーク欄をぬりつぶしなさい。

Hamilton Art Museum News

● **Special Exhibition**
The special exhibition of paintings by Canadian artists from the 19th and 20th century has just started!
Admission:
Adults: $2.00
Students: $1.00
Seniors (60 & over): Free

大問4，5

ライティング（Eメール，英作文）〈2問〉

英語のQUESTIONについて，あなたの意見とその理由を2つ，英文で書く問題です。語数の目安は25～35語。マークシート方式ではなく，記述式で答えます。

2024年度から新たにEメールの返信を書く問題が加わりました。語数の目安は15～25語で，相手からの質問への返答を書きます。

ライティング　（Eメール）

● あなたは，外国人の友達（Jane）から以下のEメールを受け取りました。Eメールを読み，それに対する返信メールを，□に英文で書きなさい。
● あなたが書く返信メールの中で，友達（Jane）からの2つの質問（下線部）に対応する内容を，あなた自身で自由に考えて答えなさい。
● あなたが書く返信メールの中で□に書く英文の語数の目安は，15語～25語です。
● 解答は，解答用紙のEメール解答欄に書きなさい。なお，解答欄の外に書かれたものは採点されません。
● 解答が友達（Jane）のEメールに対応していないと判断された場合は，0点と採点されることがあります。友達（Jane）のEメールの内容をよく読んでから答えてください。
● □の下のBest wishes,の後にあなたの名前を書く必要はありません。

Hi,

Your little sister is so cute! I saw her at the supermarket with your mother today. How old is she? Do you have any other brothers or sisters? I

リスニング 約25分，30問

第1部

会話の応答文選択〈10問〉

イラストを見ながら対話を聞き，そのあとに続く応答を選択肢から選ぶ問題です。対話と選択肢は印刷されておらず，一度しか放送されません。

第1部

No. 1 TR 14

No. 2 TR 15

第2部

会話の内容一致選択〈10問〉

対話と，その内容に関する質問を聞き，その答えとしてもっとも正しいものを選択肢から選ぶ問題です。対話と質問は印刷されておらず，選択肢は印刷されています。対話と質問は二度ずつ放送されます。

第2部

No. 11 TR 25
1 Korean.
2 Chinese.
3 Japanese.
4 Italian.

No. 12 TR 26
1 At 8:55.
2 At 9:00.
3 At 9:55.
4 At 10:00.

No. 13 TR 27
1 10 minutes.
2 40 minutes.
3 60 minutes.
4 70 minutes.

No. 14 TR 28
1 He can't find his table.
2 He didn't drink coffee.
3 He lost his watch.
4 He couldn't sleep last night.

第3部

文の内容一致選択〈10問〉

英文と，その内容に関する質問を聞き，その答えとしてもっとも正しいものを選択肢から選ぶ問題です。英文と質問は印刷されておらず，選択肢は印刷されています。英文と質問は二度ずつ放送されます。

第3部

No. 21 TR 36
1 Her father.
2 Her mother.
3 Her brother.
4 Her friends.

No. 22 TR 37
1 Last Friday.
2 Last Saturday.
3 This morning.
4 This afternoon.

No. 23 TR 38
1 Once.
2 Twice.
3 Three times.
4 Four times.

No. 24 TR 39
1 Five.
2 Six.
3 Eight.
4 Nine.

面接 約5分

与えられる問題カードに書かれている英文を音読します。その後，面接委員からされる5つの質問に，英語で答えます。
詳しい内容はP110に書いてありますので，参考にしてください。

Libraries

A lot of cities and towns in Japan have libraries. People can read or borrow many different kinds of books there, so libraries are popular places to visit. At some libraries, volunteers read some interesting stories to children.

PART 1

よく出る名詞①

学校・スポーツ

学習日

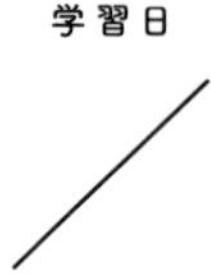

★理解度
□カンペキ!
□もう一度
□まだまだ…

英検３級では，学校に関する話題が多く出題されます。単語を「学校」「スポーツ」などのグループに分けて覚えましょう。

学校

スポーツ

(　　　　)
初心者

(　　　　)
賞

(　　　　)
ユニフォーム，制服

My単語メモ

□
□
□
□
□

	スポーツ選手		主将，船長	coach	コーチ，指導者
contest	コンテスト	field	競技場，畑	goal	ゴール，目標
injury	負傷	locker	ロッカー		練習
	スタジアム	tournament	試合，トーナメント	winner	勝利者，優勝者

練習問題

答えは別冊P1

次の *(1)* から *(6)* までの（　　）に入れるのに最も適切なものを**1**,**2**,**3**,**4**の中から一つ選びなさい。

(1) Jim really likes to watch soccer games, so he often goes to the (　　).

1 library　**2** stadium　**3** museum　**4** zoo

①②③④

(2) My sister is going to finish high school and go to (　　) this year.

1 university　**2** garden　**3** living room　**4** gym

①②③④

(3) *A:* Can I use your (　　)? I need to look up some words now.
B: Sure. Here you are.

1 eraser　**2** camera
3 information　**4** dictionary

①②③④

(4) *A:* I hear your team won a soccer tournament yesterday.
B: Yes. Our new coach gave good (　　) to us.

1 weather　**2** area　**3** advice　**4** instrument

①②③④

(5) *Girl:* A student from Australia will join our class next week.
Boy: (　　)
Girl: Mr. Taylor told us about her yesterday.

1 How do you know that?　**2** Where is the student from?
3 Did you see the student?　**4** When did you do that?

①②③④

(6) *Boy:* Yesterday, you practiced tennis all day.
Girl: I have an important match tomorrow. I'm so nervous.
Boy: (　　) I'm sure you'll do well.

1 Same to you.　**2** How was the match?
3 Don't worry.　**4** That's right.

①②③④

PART 2

よく出る名詞②

エンターテインメント・食べ物

学習日

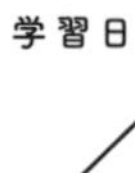

★理解度
□カンペキ!
□もう一度
□まだまだ…

My単語メモ
□
□
□
□
□
□

エンターテインメント

beach
(　　　　)

panda
(　　　　)

zoo
(　　　　)

band	(音楽の)バンド		コンサート	event	イベント
festival	祭り	fun	楽しいこと	movie	映画
	美術館,博物館	nature	自然		劇場,映画館

	動物	chimpanzee	チンパンジー	elephant	
kitten		puppy	子犬	tiger	トラ

食べ物

練習問題

答えは別冊P1

次の *(1)* から *(6)* までの（　　）に入れるのに最も適切なものを**1**,**2**,**3**,**4**の中から一つ選びなさい。

(1) John has a piano concert next week, so he is practicing very hard for the (　　).

1 environment　**2** performance
3 difference　**4** communication

①②③④

(2) My sister and I like dogs very much. Playing with them makes (　　) happy.

1 we　**2** our　**3** us　**4** ours

①②③④

(3) *A:* How did you like the movie, Ellen?
B: Well, the actors were great, but the story was (　　).

1 loud　**2** kind　**3** boring　**4** clever

①②③④

(4) *A:* Do you do anything good for your (　　)?
B: Yes. It is my habit to walk with my dog before breakfast.

1 tradition　**2** health　**3** mistakes　**4** accident

①②③④

(5) *Teacher:* Do you have any plans for the winter vacation, Tom?
Boy: Yes. (　　) Hawaii.
Teacher: Oh, lucky you.

1 You can visit　**2** I'm from
3 I'm going to　**4** I'm sure you'll like

①②③④

(6) *Boy:* Let's go to the bakery near my house in the afternoon.
Girl: Sure. What time should we meet?
Boy: (　　)

1 I'm busy in the morning.　**2** Come to my house at three.
3 What do you want to buy?　**4** I don't know where it is.

①②③④

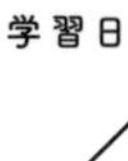

PART 3

よく出る動詞①

活動する・コミュニケーションをとる

学習日 ／

★理解度
□カンペキ！
□もう一度
□まだまだ…

「活動する」動詞

３級では使われる動詞の種類が多くなります。自分で実際に活動している様子を思い浮かべてみましょう。

（　　　　）
～を運ぶ

（　　　　）
～をきれいにする

（　　　　）
～を見る，～に会う

arrive	到着する		(～を)決める		育つ，～を育てる
jump	跳ぶ	learn	～を学ぶ	make	～を作る
	移り住む，動く	push	～を押す		～を置く
relax	くつろぐ		～を投げる	work	(機械が)作動する，働く

「コミュニケーションをとる」動詞

コミュニケーションでは積極的に相手にかかわることもあれば，自分が楽しんだり，相手を思いやったりする場合もあります。それぞれの単語について，自分が最近した行動を思い出してみましょう。

call
～に電話をする

（　　　　）
～を楽しむ

（　　　　）
待つ

	～を祝う	contact	～に連絡をとる	give	(～に)…を与える
guess	推測する		～を招待する		～に参加する
	(～に)…を見せる	take	～を連れていく	tell	～に話す，～を教える

My単語メモ
□
□
□

覚えよう
〈make＋人＋形容詞〉で「人を～にさせる」

覚えよう
take「（時間）がかかる」
cost「（お金）がかかる」

練習問題

答えは別冊P2

次の *(1)* から *(6)* までの（　　）に入れるのに最も適切なものを**1**,**2**,**3**,**4**の中から一つ選びなさい。

(1) I like this song. It always (　　) me happy.

1 thinks　**2** takes　**3** makes　**4** tells

①②③④

(2) I (　　) my camera at home, so I can't take a picture right now.

1 left　**2** got　**3** bought　**4** watched

①②③④

(3) *A:* Look. There is a notice on the door of the shop.

B: Well, it (　　), "We are closed today."

1 sells　**2** says　**3** joins　**4** buys

①②③④

(4) *A:* What should I say when I start my speech?

B: For example, "Hello everyone. Let me (　　) myself."

1 watch　**2** decide　**3** invite　**4** introduce

①②③④

(5) *Girl:* Have you read that book?

Boy: No, not yet, but (　　).

Girl: Maybe you can borrow it again.

1 I have to return it to the library today

2 I really liked it because it was interesting

3 my mother bought it for me

4 he wrote it fifty years ago

①②③④

(6) *Man:* I'd like to send this package to Hokkaido. When will it arrive?

Woman: (　　)

1 It costs 2,000 yen.　**2** The train will start at five p.m.

3 It takes three days.　**4** You should take a taxi.

①②③④

PART 4

よく出る動詞②
気持ちを表す

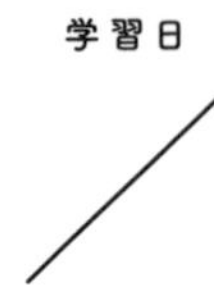

気持ちを表す動詞

( )	( )	( )
～を見つける，～とわかる	望む	においがする

believe	(～を)信じる	expect	～を予期する
	～を感じる		～を必要とする
taste	～の味がする		～を理解する

反対の意味とセットで覚える動詞

次の動詞は，反対の意味の動詞とセットで覚えると記憶に残りやすく，

思い出しやすくなります。

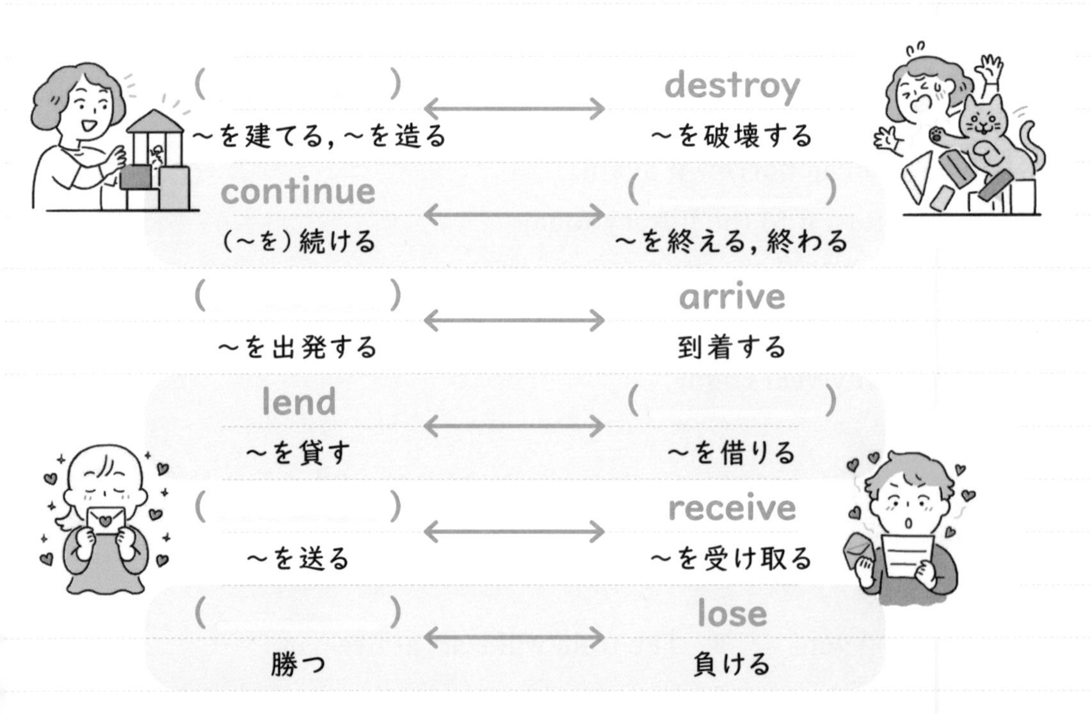

( ) ～を建てる，～を造る	⟷	destroy ～を破壊する
continue (～を)続ける	⟷	( ) ～を終える，終わる
( ) ～を出発する	⟷	arrive 到着する
lend ～を貸す	⟷	( ) ～を借りる
( ) ～を送る	⟷	receive ～を受け取る
( ) 勝つ	⟷	lose 負ける

My単語メモ

□

□

□

□

□

□

練習問題

答えは別冊 P2

次の *(1)* から *(6)* までの（　　）に入れるのに最も適切なものを **1**,**2**,**3**,**4** の中から一つ選びなさい。

(1) Judy spoke English quickly, so I couldn't (　　) her words.

1 understand　**2** run　**3** mean　**4** throw　①②③④

(2) *A:* I have my final high school match tomorrow.

B: You have practiced hard for three years. I (　　) you can win.

1 listen　**2** believe　**3** try　**4** fight　①②③④

(3) *A:* How are you (　　) this morning, Nancy?

B: Much better, Mom. I think I can go to school today.

1 taking　**2** reading　**3** showing　**4** feeling　①②③④

(4) *A:* Mark's birthday is coming soon. Don't forget to buy a present for him.

B: Thanks, I'll (　　) that.

1 go　**2** remember　**3** miss　**4** ask　①②③④

(5) *Woman:* (　　) You don't look well, Fred.

Man: I was very busy all day, so I'm a little tired.

Woman: Please take a rest.

1 What are you doing?　**2** Sounds good.

3 What's wrong?　**4** Good luck.　①②③④

(6) *Girl:* Bob, what do you think of my new dress?

Boy: (　　)

Girl: Thank you.

1 The color really suits you.　**2** Where did you go?

3 I don't know the name of it.　**4** I'll check the website.　①②③④

PART 5

よく出る熟語①

get, takeを使った熟語

学習日

★理解度
□カンペキ!
□もう一度
□まだまだ…

いくつかの語がセットになっているのが熟語です。基本の動詞getとtakeを使った熟語を覚えましょう。

My単語メモ
□
□
□
□
□
□

getを使った熟語

getの基本の意味は「得る」です。

get (　　　　) 寒くなる

get (　　　　) 空腹になる

get on (~) 乗り物などに(　　　　)

get 　　　from ~	~から逃げる,~を離れる	get	暗くなる
get home	帰宅する	get off (~)	(乗り物などを)
get to ~	~に着く	get well	(体調が)よくなる
get along with ~	~とうまくやる	get ~ a ride	~を車で送る

takeを使った熟語

takeの基本の意味は「取る」です。

take a (　　　　) 休憩する

take a (　　　　) 写真を撮る

take care of your dog あなたの犬の(　　　　)をする

take a walk	
dance lessons	ダンスのレッスンを受ける
take me to the amusement park	私を遊園地に　　　　いく
take part in the hiking	ハイキングに　　　　する
Our plane will 　　　off soon.	私たちの飛行機は間もなく離陸します。
It took me 2 hours to get home.	私は帰宅するのに2時間かかりました。

練習問題

答えは別冊P3

次の *(1)* から *(6)* までの（　　）に入れるのに最も適切なものを**1**,**2**,**3**,**4**の中から一つ選びなさい。

(1) Please (　　) off the light when you leave the room.

1 stop　**2** turn　**3** get　**4** change　①②③④

(2) Ms. Smith is going to (　　) part in the meeting this afternoon.

1 go　**2** join　**3** enter　**4** take　①②③④

(3) *A:* What is your dream?

B: When I grow (　　), I want to be a professional soccer player.

1 on　**2** over　**3** up　**4** in　①②③④

(4) *A:* Did you (　　) from Kevin?

B: No. I'm still waiting for his e-mail.

1 hear　**2** send　**3** see　**4** listen　①②③④

(5) *Girl:* How's your life in a new town?

Boy: Good. My neighbors are kind to me, and (　　).

1 I'll visit there again next year

2 I haven't seen them yet

3 I'm getting along with them

4 I wasn't able to get there　①②③④

(6) *Boy:* You were looking for your textbook. Did you find it?

Girl: Yes, I did. (　　)

1 It was in another bag.

2 I couldn't see it anywhere.

3 I could buy a nice bag.

4 I don't think it's interesting.　①②③④

PART 6

よく出る熟語②

goを使った熟語，量を表す熟語

学習日

★理解度
□カンペキ！
□もう一度
□まだまだ…

いくつかの語がセットになっているのが熟語です。基本の動詞goを使った熟語と，「量を表す熟語」を覚えましょう。

goを使った熟語

goの基本の意味は「行く」です。

go on a trip
(　　　　)に出かける

go to (　　　　)
寝る

go for a walk	に行く
shopping	買い物に行く
go straight	まっすぐに行く
go to the doctor	医師に診てもらいに行く

量を表す熟語

water（水）は形のない液体なので，１つ，２つとは数えません（sをつけて複数形にしません）。数えられない名詞を「不可算名詞」といいます。なんとbread（パン）も不可算名詞です。パンはどんな形でも存在できますし，いくら切ってもパンだからです。水はグラスに入った形，パンは切った形で数えます。

a few ～	2，3の～
a glass of ～	グラス１杯の～
a lot of ～	多くの～
a number of ～	多くの～，多数の～
a piece of ～	ひと切れの～

My単語メモ
□
□
□
□
□
□

注意！
see a doctor
「医者に行く」
とも言います

覚えよう
milk（牛乳）や
coffee（コーヒー）
などの飲み物や，
paper（紙）なども
不可算名詞です

練習問題

答えは別冊P3

次の *(1)* から *(6)* までの（　　）に入れるのに最も適切なものを**1**,**2**,**3**,**4**の中から一つ選びなさい。

(1) At (　　), we thought the job was too difficult for us, but now we can do it well.

1 once　**2** first　**3** least　**4** last　①②③④

(2) I always buy a cup of coffee on my (　　) to work.

1 time　**2** place　**3** road　**4** way　①②③④

(3) *A:* Did you see Mr. Wilson?

B: Yes, he ran out of the office just now. He looked busy (　　) usual.

1 on　**2** for　**3** as　**4** by　①②③④

(4) *A:* I want to be a movie director in the future.

B: I hope your dream will come (　　).

1 true　**2** right　**3** good　**4** back　①②③④

(5) *Man:* My son is five years old. He remembers almost all national flags.

Woman: That's great. (　　)

1 He may have a cold.

2 He has a good memory.

3 He had a good time with you.

4 He has never been there.　①②③④

(6) *Mother:* Bob, I want to carry these boxes to my car. (　　)

Son: OK, Mom. I'll carry them all.

1 I can't give you a ride.

2 We have to get on the bus.

3 Will you give me a hand?

4 Please take off your hat.　①②③④

PART 7

比較
比べる文

学習日

★理解度
□カンペキ！
□もう一度
□まだまだ…

PART7からは文法の問題に入ります。

考えてみよう 次の３人の中で，一番背が高いのはだれか英語で書きましょう。（　　　　　）

① 原級 Mike is as tall (　　　　) Jim. マイクはジムと同じくらい背が高い。

-er, -estがつかない元の形

② 比較級 Nancy is (　　　　) than Mike. ナンシーはマイクよりも背が高い。

比較級（-er）＋than＋比べる人

③ 最上級 Nancy is the (　　　　) of the three.

最上級（-est）＋of や in

ナンシーは3人の中で最も背が高い。

よく出る形容詞の，比較級・最上級の形を覚えましょう。

基本の変化 比較級は-er，最上級は-estをつけます。

原級	比較級	最上級
long（長い）		longest
tall（背が高い）	taller	

長い語の変化 -er，-estをつけると長すぎて発音しにくいので，前にmore，mostをつけます。

原級	比較級	最上級
beautiful（美しい）		most beautiful
expensive（高価な）	more expensive	

不規則な変化 一つ一つ覚えておきましょう。

原級	比較級	最上級
good（良い），well（上手に）		
bad（悪い），ill（病気の）		
many（数が多い），much（量が多い）		
little（少ない）		

覚えよう

よく出題されるので，しっかり覚えよう

練習問題

答えは別冊P4

次の *(1)* から *(6)* までの（　　）に入れるのに最も適切なものを**1**,**2**,**3**,**4**の中から一つ選びなさい。

(1) This winter was (　　) than last winter, so there was almost no snow.

1 warm　**2** warmer　**3** warmest　**4** as warm　①②③④

(2) Helping each other is the (　　) important thing of all.

1 right　**2** so　**3** more　**4** most　①②③④

(3) *A:* Will you play tennis with me?
B: I'd love to, but I can't play as well (　　) you.
A: That's OK. We'll have a good time.

1 as　**2** than　**3** in　**4** for　①②③④

(4) *A:* How was the musical you saw yesterday?
B: It's the (　　) one I have ever seen.

1 good　**2** better　**3** best　**4** most　①②③④

(5) *Boy:* Making pizza seems difficult.
Girl: It's not too hard. (　　)
Boy: Then I want to try to make it. Please tell me how to do it.

1 It's easier than making cake for me.
2 We have to buy a lot of food to make it.
3 I know a good restaurant near my house.
4 It was so hard that I gave up making it.　①②③④

(6) *Mother:* Let's go shopping, Mary. (　　)
Mary: OK, I'm coming, Mom.

1 It's snowing, so we can't go out.
2 See you later.
3 Get ready as soon as possible.
4 You are too busy to go with me.　①②③④

PART 8

過去形と現在完了形

動詞の形に注意する

学習日

★理解度
□カンペキ!
□もう一度
□まだまだ…

3級を受験するみなさんが難しいと感じる文法の一つに,「過去形」と「現在完了形」の違いがあります。

過去形

現在から切り離された過去を表します。

Cathy **went** to the shopping mall last week.
（went：動詞の過去形）

キャシーは先週ショッピングモールに行きました。

「過去のある時点」で,キャシーがショッピングモールに行ったことを表しています。「現在」についてはわかりません。

覚えよう

否定文は〈have／has not＋過去分詞〉

現在完了形〈have／has＋過去分詞〉

「現在」に影響を与えている「過去」を表します。

1 「～してしまった」 動作の完了,その結果としての現在の状態を表します。

My uncle (　　　　) (　　　　) to England on business.
（〈has＋過去分詞〉）

おじは仕事でイギリスに行ってしまいました。

2 「ずっと～している」 現在までの継続を表します。

They have been (　　　　) for ten years.
（have been：〈have＋過去分詞〉　for ten years：「10年間」）

彼らは10年間ずっと結婚しています(＝結婚してから10年になります)。

注意!

have gone to「～へ行ってしまった」

have been to「～へ行ったことがある」

現在完了形(継続)の文には,下のような期間を表す語がつきます。

for ten years	10年間	since 2010	2010年以来

3 「～したことがある」 現在までの経験を表します。

I (　　　　) (　　　　) this book many times.
（〈have＋過去分詞〉）

この本を何度も読んだことがあります。

練習問題

答えは別冊P4

次の *(1)* から *(6)* までの（　　）に入れるのに最も適切なものを**1**,**2**,**3**,**4**の中から一つ選びなさい。

(1) Jim has already (　　) his room.

1 clean　**2** cleans　**3** cleaned　**4** cleaning　①②③④

(2) Here is a photo that my father (　　) in Kyoto last month.

1 takes　**2** take　**3** took　**4** taken　①②③④

(3) *A:* Have you ever (　　) to London?

B: Yes, twice.

1 go　**2** went　**3** were　**4** been　①②③④

(4) *A:* Your brother looks like a college student, (　　) he?

B: Really? In fact he's a high school student.

1 does　**2** doesn't　**3** is　**4** isn't　①②③④

(5) *Girl:* What were you doing when I called you last night?

Boy: (　　) So, I couldn't answer the phone.

1 I didn't watch TV after dinner.

2 I was taking a bath.

3 I'm sorry, but I'll be late.

4 I have not eaten dinner yet.　①②③④

(6) *Boy:* I'm enjoying my stay in Japan. I love Tokyo.

Girl: That's good. (　　)

Boy: It's been a week.

1 How long have you stayed in Tokyo?

2 When will you go back to Australia?

3 Where are you staying now?

4 What do you want to do during your stay?　①②③④

PART 9

進行形

現在進行形と過去進行形

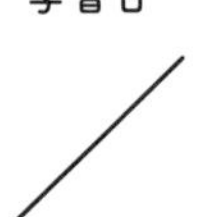
学習日

★理解度
□カンペキ!
□もう一度
□まだまだ…

現在進行形「～しています」 be動詞（am, is, are）のあとに，動詞のing形を続けると「現在進行形」を表します。現在進行形とは「今，進行している動作」のことで，「～しています」という意味になります。

現在進行形 I (　　　　) watching TV now.
〈be動詞+動詞のing形〉
私は今テレビを見ています。

現在進行形 Mark (　　　　) (　　　　) the piano.
マークはピアノを演奏しています。

否定文 I am (　　　　) watching TV now.
私は今テレビを見ていません。

疑問文 (　　　　) Mark playing the piano?
マークはピアノを演奏していますか。

覚えよう
疑問文はbe動詞を前に出します

過去進行形「～していました」 be動詞の過去形（was, were）のあとに，動詞のing形を続けると「過去進行形」を表します。過去進行形とは「過去に進行中だった動作」のことで，「～していました」という意味になります。

過去進行形 My mother (　　　　) cooking breakfast for me.
〈be動詞の過去形+動詞のing形〉
母は私のために朝食を作っていました。

否定文 My mother was (　　　　) cooking breakfast for me.
母は私のために朝食を作っていませんでした。

疑問文 (　　　　) my mother cooking breakfast for me?
母は私のために朝食を作っていましたか。

練習問題

答えは別冊P5

次の **(1)** から **(6)** までの（　　）に入れるのに最も適切なものを**1**,**2**,**3**,**4**の中から一つ選びなさい。

(1) Please turn down the radio. A baby (　　) now.

1 is sleeping　　**2** is slept

3 was sleeping　　**4** was slept　　①②③④

(2) When I was (　　) in the park, it began to rain suddenly.

1 walk　**2** walked　**3** walking　**4** to walk　　①②③④

(3) *A:* What (　　) you reading now, Ken? Is it an English textbook?

B: No, it's a comic book written in English. It's easy for me.

1 are　**2** do　**3** did　**4** can　　①②③④

(4) *A:* Where are you (　　), Mark? I can give you a ride to the station.

B: Thank you, Ms. Brown. I have to take the 9 p.m. train.

1 go　**2** going　**3** went　**4** to go　　①②③④

(5) *Mother:* You talked with Kyoko on the phone too long. (　　)

Jane: Sorry, Mom. She asked me about her English homework.

1 Did you leave a message?

2 Who is this speaking?

3 Where did you meet her?

4 What were you talking about?　　①②③④

(6) *Boy:* I saw you in front of the theater at three last Sunday.

Girl: You did? (　　) We enjoyed a play and dinner at the restaurant that day.

1 I didn't go out last Sunday.

2 I was waiting for my friend then.

3 What time will you be there?

4 That's impossible.　　①②③④

PART 10 未来

willとbe going to ～

学習日

★理解度
□カンペキ!
□もう一度
□まだまだ…

未来を表す表現には，willとbe going to ～があります。

willの意味：客観的なこれから起こる出来事「～でしょう」，
自分の意思「～するつもり」
be going to ～の意味：自分が「～する予定です，きっと～しそうです」

違いを理解しておこう

willを使った未来の表現「～でしょう」「～するつもり」

未来の文を作るときにはwillを置き，動詞は原形にします。動詞がbe動詞（am, is, are）の場合は，原形のbeになります。

現在形 He is rich. 彼はお金持ちです。

未来 He will (　　　　) rich someday. 彼はいつかお金持ちになるでしょう。
〈will+動詞の原形〉

未来 I (　　　　) drive you to the station.
駅まで車で送るつもりです[送ってあげるよ]。

覚えよう
will notを短縮してwon'tになります

未来の文は，tomorrow（明日に），in the future（将来に）などの未来を表す語句と一緒に使うことが多いです。

否定文 He (　　　　) be rich. 彼はお金持ちにならないでしょう。

疑問文 (　　　　) he be rich someday? 彼はいつかお金持ちになるでしょうか。

be going to ～を使った未来の表現「～する予定です」

be going toのあとには，動詞の原形を続けます。

現在形 I stay home. 私は家にいます。

未来 I (　　　　) (　　　　) (　　　　) stay home tomorrow.
動詞の原形
私は明日，家にいる予定です。

否定文 I am (　　　　) going to stay home tomorrow.
私は明日，家にいる予定ではありません。

疑問文 (　　　　) you going to stay home tomorrow?
あなたは明日，家にいる予定ですか。

練習問題

答えは別冊P5

次の *(1)* から *(6)* までの（　　）に入れるのに最も適切なものを**1**,**2**,**3**,**4**の中から一つ選びなさい。

(1) Where (　　) you go if it rains tomorrow?

1 have　**2** will　**3** are　**4** did

①②③④

(2) My sister is going (　　) abroad next year.

1 studies　**2** study　**3** to study　**4** will study

①②③④

(3) *A:* Will you go fishing on Sunday?

B: No, I (　　). I have a lot of work to do this weekend.

1 don't　**2** won't　**3** haven't　**4** wasn't

①②③④

(4) *A:* I made a perfect plan for my trip to Hokkaido.

B: (　　) you going to ski there?

A: Of course.

1 Do　**2** Will　**3** Did　**4** Are

①②③④

(5) *Boy:* What are you going to do this summer vacation?

Girl: (　　), but I'd like to try something new.

1 I haven't decided yet　**2** I enjoyed swimming

3 It was boring　**4** We had a wonderful time

①②③④

(6) *Teacher:* Tell me what your dream for the future is.

Student: I want to help sick people, so (　　).

1 it was difficult for me

2 there isn't a hospital

3 I'll become a nurse

4 I'm looking for a good teacher

①②③④

PART 11

不定詞・動名詞

「～すること」

学習日

★理解度
□カンペキ！
□もう一度
□まだまだ…

不定詞〈to＋動詞の原形〉

〈to＋動詞の原形〉には，「～すること」「～するための」「～するために」の意味があります。

❶「～すること」 名詞のはたらき

To (　　　　) English is very exciting.

〈to+動詞の原形〉「～すること」

英語を勉強することはとてもわくわくします。

❷「～するための」 形容詞のはたらき（前の名詞・代名詞を修飾します）

Do you want anything (　　　　) drink?

〈to+動詞の原形〉「～するための」

飲むための何か（=何か飲み物）はいかがですか。

❸「～するために」 副詞のはたらき（前の動詞を修飾します）

He worked hard (　　　　) give her a good education.

〈to+動詞の原形〉「～するために」

彼は彼女によい教育を与えるために頑張って働きました。

動名詞〈動詞のing形〉

〈動詞のing形〉で，「～すること」と訳します。

I finished cleaning my room.　私は部屋をそうじすることを終えました。

動詞のing形

動名詞があとに続く動詞

~ing	～することを楽しむ
~ing	～することを終える（=～し終える）
~ing	～することをやめる

不定詞があとに続く動詞

to ～	～したい
to ～	～することを願う
to ～	～することを決意する
to ～	～することが必要だ

覚えよう

動名詞が続く動詞，
不定詞が続く動詞は
しっかり整理して覚えよう

練習問題

答えは別冊P6

次の *(1)* から *(6)* までの（　　）に入れるのに最も適切なものを**1**,**2**,**3**,**4**の中から一つ選びなさい。

(1) Ken's father told him (　　) his mother more often.

1 helps　**2** helped　**3** to help　**4** helping　①②③④

(2) Lucy was angry, so she left the room without (　　) goodbye.

1 to say　**2** says　**3** said　**4** saying　①②③④

(3) *A:* It's necessary for us (　　) something good for the environment.

B: I agree with you. Let's talk more about it.

1 do　**2** to do　**3** doing　**4** to doing　①②③④

(4) *A:* I will leave Japan, but I will keep (　　) Japanese.

B: I'm glad to hear that. Let's speak Japanese on the phone.

1 study　**2** to study　**3** studying　**4** studies　①②③④

(5) *Mother:* Lisa, are you going to join the party tonight?

Girl: Yes, but (　　)

Mother: OK. Let's choose together. How about that red one?

1 I don't know where I should go.
2 I don't know what to wear.
3 please tell me what time it starts.
4 my friend Karen will not come.　①②③④

(6) *Boy:* How was the summer festival yesterday?

Girl: It was nice. (　　)

Boy: Wow, it's *bon-odori*. Sounds fun.

1 It was raining, so we couldn't go out.
2 I hear many people will come to the shrine.
3 I cleaned the park as a volunteer.
4 We enjoyed dancing in a circle.　①②③④

PART 12

関係代名詞

関係代名詞の種類とはたらき

学習日 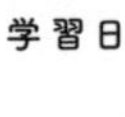

★理解度
□カンペキ！
□もう一度
□まだまだ…

関係代名詞には「接続詞」のように，2つの文をつないで1つの文にするはたらきがあります。また，「(代)名詞」のように，あとの節の中で主語や目的語になります。

関係代名詞の種類

先行詞＼役割	主格	所有格	目的格
人	**who**	**whose**	**whom(who)**
物事	**which**	**whose**	**which**
人・物事	**that**	—	**that**

① 主格の関係代名詞のはたらき

I know the girl. ＋ She is from Italy.

私は女の子を知っています。 彼女はイタリア出身です。

I know the girl ( ) is from Italy.

先行詞「人」 関係代名詞

私はイタリア出身の女の子を知っています。

覚えよう

who以下が the girlを修飾しています

② 所有格の関係代名詞のはたらき

I know the girl. ＋ Her father is a dentist.

私は女の子を知っています。 彼女の父親は歯医者です。

I know the girl ( ) father is a dentist.

先行詞「人」 関係代名詞

私は父親が歯医者である女の子を知っています。

③ 目的格の関係代名詞のはたらき

This is the movie. ＋ I saw it last night.

これは映画です。 私は昨夜それを見ました。

This is the movie ( ) I saw last night.

先行詞「物」 関係代名詞

これは私が昨夜見た映画です。

注意！

目的格の関係代名詞は省略できます

練習問題

答えは別冊P6

次の *(1)* から *(6)* までの（　　）に入れるのに最も適切なものを**1**,**2**,**3**,**4**の中から一つ選びなさい。

(1) I have a friend (　　) lives in London.

1 who　**2** whose　**3** which　**4** where　①②③④

(2) I have a classmate (　　) father is a professional soccer player.

1 who　**2** whose　**3** which　**4** what　①②③④

(3) *A:* Is there any good restaurants (　　) serve Japanese food?
B: I hear a new sushi restaurant opened. We should try.

1 who　**2** whose　**3** which　**4** how　①②③④

(4) *A:* Did you like this movie?
B: Yes. It's the most interesting movie (　　) I have ever seen.

1 that　**2** what　**3** of　**4** before　①②③④

(5) *Man:* Do you know a person who speaks French?
Woman: Yes. (　　)

1 Where is he from?　**2** I've been there once.
3 How did you learn it?　**4** John is good at it.　①②③④

(6) *Boy:* Yesterday I went to a soccer stadium. How about you, Lucy?
Girl: I went shopping with Kate. (　　)
Boy: It's very beautiful and suits you.

1 This is a necklace I bought yesterday.
2 I'm looking forward to going with her.
3 Was the game exciting?
4 How will the weather be this weekend?　①②③④

PART 13

受け身

受動態の基本

学習日

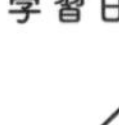

★理解度
□カンペキ!
□もう一度
□まだまだ…

受け身の文は「～される」「～された」という意味を表し，文の形は〈be動詞(am, is, are, was, were)＋過去分詞〉です。

注意!

be動詞は，主語や時制に合わせて使い分けよう

通常の文 「(人／物) が～する」というように，行為をする人／物が主語です。

Karen ( ) the letter **last week.** 先週カレンがその手紙を書きました。

受け身の文(受動態) 「(人／物) によって～される」というように，行為をされる人／物が主語になります。

The letter ( ) ( ) **by** Karen **last week.**

〈be動詞＋過去分詞〉 過去を表す語句

先週その手紙はカレンによって書かれました。

動詞の活用

- 過去形・過去分詞が同じ形　**buy**(～を買う) － **bought** － **bought**
- 原形・過去形・過去分詞がすべて同じ形　**cut**(～を切る) － **cut** － **cut**
- 原形・過去形・過去分詞がすべて違う形

原形	過去形	過去分詞
be (～である)	**was／were**	
break (～を壊す)	**broke**	
eat (～を食べる)	**ate**	
do (～をする)	**did**	
drive (～を運転する)	**drove**	
give (～を与える)	**gave**	
go (行く)	**went**	
know (～を知っている)	**knew**	
speak (話す)	**spoke**	
take (～を取る)	**took**	

覚えよう

過去形と過去分詞が違う動詞はよく出題されます

練習問題

答えは別冊P7

次の *(1)* から *(6)* までの（　　）に入れるのに最も適切なものを**1**,**2**,**3**,**4**の中から一つ選びなさい。

(1) French and English are (　　) in this country.

1 speaking　**2** speak　**3** spoke　**4** spoken　①②③④

(2) Science is (　　) by Ms. Ito twice a week.

1 teach　**2** taught　**3** teaching　**4** teaches　①②③④

(3) *A:* My bike was (　　) yesterday. I'm sad.

B: You should go to a police station.

1 steal　**2** stole　**3** stolen　**4** stealing　①②③④

(4) *A:* It snowed last night, didn't it?

B: Yes, I was surprised. When I got up, the ground was covered (　　) snow.

1 for　**2** with　**3** at　**4** on　①②③④

(5) *Girl:* When was this temple built?

Boy: (　　)

1 About 400 years ago.

2 We can visit here anytime.

3 About 300 people a day.

4 I went there by train.　①②③④

(6) *Girl:* Will you help me, Ken?

Boy: Sure. What's the matter, Judy?

Girl: (　　), so I can't read it.

1 The bookstore is close

2 I want to write an interesting story

3 I will take piano lessons

4 This letter is written in Japanese　①②③④

PART 14

分詞

現在分詞，過去分詞のはたらき

学習日

★理解度
□カンペキ！
□もう一度
□まだまだ…

３級に出題される〈-ing形〉と〈-ed形〉はどちらも動詞が変化した形です。これらはそれぞれ「現在分詞」「過去分詞」と呼ばれ，形容詞としてはたらきます。

「形容詞としてはたらく」とは，前からも後ろからも名詞を修飾するということです。

現在分詞（-ing形）「～する／～している」

前から修飾　1語で名詞を修飾するとき

That was an (　　　　　) movie.

現在分詞→名詞

あれはおもしろい映画でした。

後ろから修飾　〈現在分詞＋語句〉で名詞を修飾するとき

A car (　　　　　) five people stopped at the intersection.

名詞←〈現在分詞＋語句〉

5人を乗せた車が交差点で停車しました。

過去分詞（-ed形）「～される／～されている」

前から修飾　1語で名詞を修飾するとき

There is a (　　　　　) clock.

過去分詞→名詞

壊された時計があります。

後ろから修飾　〈過去分詞＋語句〉で名詞を修飾するとき

There is a clock (　　　　　) by Laura.

名詞←〈過去分詞＋語句〉

ローラによって壊された時計があります。

覚えよう

短い（1語）ときは前から，長い（2語以上）ときは後ろから名詞を修飾します

注意！

過去分詞は，PART13の表で確認しよう

練習問題

答えは別冊P7

次の *(1)* から *(6)* までの（　　）に入れるのに最も適切なものを**1**,**2**,**3**,**4**の中から一つ選びなさい。

(1) My father wants to buy a car (　　　) in Japan.

1 make　**2** makes　**3** made　**4** making　①②③④

(2) Who is the boy (　　　) with Mr. Kato over there?

1 talk　**2** talking　**3** talked　**4** talks　①②③④

(3) *A:* These cookies (　　　) by your sister are very good.

B: Thank you. She always makes delicious sweets.

1 baked　**2** baking　**3** to bake　**4** bake　①②③④

(4) *A:* Excuse me. Where is the nearest convenience store?

B: Sorry, I don't know. Please ask the man (　　　) in front of the gate.

1 stand　**2** stood　**3** to stand　**4** standing　①②③④

(5) *Boy:* This book was interesting. (　　　)

Girl: Yes. I like all the novels written by him.

1 Tell me where you bought it.

2 When did you read it?

3 I can't remember what the title is.

4 Is the writer famous in your country?　①②③④

(6) *Ms. Brown:* Sally, do you know the student who sings well?

Girl: Yes. (　　　)

1 I'm not good at playing the piano.

2 I like listening to Japanese pop music.

3 Kyoko is the best singer in our class.

4 I know a lot of songs loved by young people.　①②③④

PART 15

会話表現①

勧誘する・何かをお願いする

学習日

★理解度
□カンペキ!
□もう一度
□まだまだ…

would likeを使った表現

勧誘・依頼の中では，would likeがよく出題されます。I would like to ～は，I want to ～の丁寧な表現です。want to ～は自分のやりたいことをストレートに伝えるのに対して，would like to ～は相手の助けを求める「もしよかったら～」のニュアンスがあります。

依頼 I (　　　　) like some tea, please.
紅茶をいただけますか。

勧誘 Would you (　　　　) to join us tonight?
今夜，仲間に加わりませんか。

勧誘・依頼に対する答え方

勧誘・依頼に対する答え方には「受ける」「断る」「どちらとも言えない」など，さまざまな正解があります。

覚えよう
答え方までセットで覚えましょう

Why don't we have dinner together?
夕食をご一緒しませんか。

Of course. いいですよ。	No problem. いいですよ。
I'd be glad to. 喜んで。	Sure, I'd love to. もちろん，喜んで。

How about calling John?
ジョンに電話してみてはどう？

Maybe next time. 次回はそうします。	My boss will help me. Thanks anyway. 上司が手助けしてくれます。ありがとうございます。

(　　　　) you like to see the house?
家をご覧になりますか。

I'm not sure. どうでしょう。	I'll have to ask my wife. 妻に聞いてみないと。

練習問題

答えは別冊P8

次の *(1)* から *(5)* までの会話について，(　　　) に入れるのに最も適切なものを **1**,**2**,**3**,**4** の中から一つ選びなさい。

(1) *Boy:* Can you tell me about your sister?
Girl: OK. (　　　　)
1 How many sisters do you have?
2 I have two dogs and a cat.
3 My sister Kate is a college student.
4 My aunt became a math teacher last year.

① ② ③ ④

(2) *Woman:* (　　　　) This room is a little hot.
Man: Yes, please. Thank you for asking.
1 Shall I open the window?
2 Do you have something to eat?
3 Do you think I have a fever?
4 Can you turn up the radio?

① ② ③ ④

(3) *Boy:* I'm going to buy a birthday present for Bob this afternoon.
Girl: Me too. (　　　　)
Boy: That's a good idea.
1 I don't know any good shops.
2 What did you buy for him?
3 Tell me how old Bob is.
4 Shall we go shopping together?

① ② ③ ④

(4) *Boy:* I forgot to bring my racket today. (　　　　)
Girl: Sorry, Alex. I have only one, and I'm using it now.
1 Will you buy one?　　**2** Can I borrow yours?
3 What are you doing?　**4** What's the problem?

① ② ③ ④

(5) *Boy:* I have two movie tickets. Why don't we go this weekend?
Girl: I'd love to, but I'm busy on Saturday. (　　　　)
Boy: All right. Sunday is fine with me.
1 I don't like a movie theater.
2 How about on Sunday?
3 Maybe next time.
4 Where will we meet on Saturday?

① ② ③ ④

PART 16

会話表現②

電話での会話

学習日 ／

★理解度
□カンペキ！
□もう一度
□まだまだ…

3級では会話問題やリスニング問題などで，電話での応答が出題されます。相手を呼び出してもらうときの表現や，相手が不在だったときの表現などを覚えておきましょう。

相手を呼び出すときの表現

電話をかける	電話を受ける
Hello, this is Wendell calling. こちらはウェンデルです。 ↓	
May I (　　　　) to Ms. White, please? ホワイトさんとお話しできますか。	➡ Sure, hold on, please. もちろんです，お待ちください。
Is Dr. Powell there? パウエル医師はいますか。	➡ Speaking. 私ですが。

相手が不在だったときの表現

電話をかける	電話を受ける
Can I talk with Melissa, please? メリッサと話せますか。	➡ Sorry, she's on another line now. すみません，彼女は他の電話にでています。
	➡ May I take a message? ご伝言を預かりましょうか。
➡ That's okay. I'll call back later. 結構です。またかけなおします。	

電話でよく出るその他の表現

Hi, Eric. What's up? もしもし，エリック。どうしたの？	Who's calling? どちら様ですか。
Just a minute, please. 少々お待ちください。	Sorry, you have the (　　　　) number. すみませんが，番号をお間違えです。

練習問題

答えは別冊P8

次の ***(1)*** から ***(4)*** までの会話について，(　　　) に入れるのに最も適切なものを**1**,**2**,**3**,**4**の中から一つ選びなさい。

(1) *Boy:* Hello. This is Bob. (　　　　　)
Girl: Speaking. What's up, Bob?
Boy: Hi, Jane. Are you free this afternoon?

1 What's your phone number?　**2** Can I speak to Jane?
3 Nice to meet you.　**4** Thank you for calling.

①②③④

(2) *Man:* Hello.
Girl: Hello, Mr. Taylor. Is Cathy home now?
Man: (　　　　　) She'll be back in an hour.

1 Yes, she is at home now.　**2** Hold on, please.
3 Sorry, but she's out now.　**4** I didn't take a message.

①②③④

(3) *Man:* Hello, this is Steve Brown. May I speak to Mr. Wilson?
Woman: He's in a meeting right now. Shall I tell him to call you back?
Man: That's OK. (　　　　　)

1 I'll call again later.　**2** Can I take a message?
3 There's a phone call for you.　**4** How about meeting at ten?

①②③④

(4) *Woman:* Hello. Is this the Green Supermarket?
Man: Sorry, but this is not a supermarket. (　　　　　)
Woman: I'm sorry. I made a mistake.

1 Tell me your phone number.
2 What do you need to buy?
3 Welcome to our store.
4 You have the wrong number.

①②③④

PART 17

会話表現③

旅行先・買い物での会話

学習日 

★理解度
□カンペキ！
□もう一度
□まだまだ…

リスニングや会話問題などでは，お店での店員と客とのやりとりも出題されます。

洋服を選ぶときの表現

店員	客
(　　　　) to our shop. May I help you? ようこそお越しくださいました。何かお探しですか。	I'm (　　　　) for a skirt. スカートを探しています。
We have some over there. How about this one? あちらにいくつかございます。これはいかがですか。	May I try this on? 試着できますか。
Certainly, ma'am. （↑男性のときはsir） I'll show you the way. もちろんです，お客様。ご案内します。	

会計するときの表現

店員	客
You look good on it. お似合いです。	How (　　　　) is this skirt? このスカートはいくらですか。
This is on sale. It's three thousand yen. セール中です。3000円です。	That's fine. I'll take this. それでいいです。これを買います。
Thank you. How would you like to (　　　　)? ありがとうございます。 お支払いはどうなさいますか。	Do you accept credit card? クレジットカードは使えますか。

練習問題

答えは別冊P9

次の *(1)* から *(5)* までの会話について，（　　）に入れるのに最も適切なものを**1**,**2**,**3**,**4**の中から一つ選びなさい。

(1) *Salesclerk:* May I help you?
Customer: (　　　) Thank you.
Salesclerk: Let me know if you need anything.

1 Where is the bus stop?　**2** I'm not sure what time it is.
3 I'm just looking.　**4** I'm glad you like it.

①②③④

(2) *Customer:* This shirt is too large for me. (　　　)
Salesclerk: Certainly. Here is a smaller one.

1 Can I try on a different size?
2 Should I decide to buy this size?
3 Do you have this in another color?
4 I think it fits me perfectly.

①②③④

(3) *Customer:* I like this bag. (　　　)
Salesclerk: It's 20 dollars.
Customer: OK. I'll take it.

1 How many bags do you have?　**2** How often do you come?
3 When did you buy it?　**4** How much is it?

①②③④

(4) *Boy:* I think we are lost, Karen. What should we do?
Girl: Take it easy, Roger. (　　　)
Boy: You're right. Here it is.

1 Let's check the map.　**2** I don't know where we are.
3 Tell me what to do.　**4** Where do you want to go?

①②③④

(5) *Boy:* There are many places to see in New York. Where should we go first?
Girl: How about the Statue of Liberty? (　　　)
Boy: No, never. I'd like to see it.

1 What do you call it?　**2** Have you ever seen it before?
3 I've just seen it.　**4** Please tell me how to get there.

①②③④

PART 18

会話表現④
レストラン・食事での会話

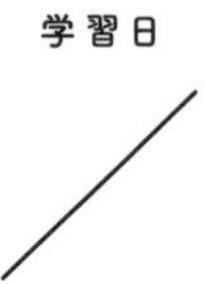

★理解度
□カンペキ!
□もう一度
□まだまだ…

レストランでの店員と客との会話も多く出題されます。注文から料理の提供まで，どんな場面かを想像しながら学習しましょう。

注文するときの表現

店員	客
Are you ready to ( ), sir? お客様，ご注文はお決まりですか。	Yes. Could I have a beef steak? はい。ステーキをいただけますか。
Sure. How would you like your steak? かしこまりました。ステーキの焼き加減はどうなさいますか。	Medium, please. ミディアムでお願いします。
Would you like a salad with that? ご一緒にサラダはいかがですか。	

食後の表現

店員	客
Here's your coffee. Do you take sugar or milk? コーヒーをお持ちしました。 お砂糖とミルクはご利用ですか。	Just a little ( ), please. 砂糖を少し入れてください。
Would you like some more ( )? パンをまだ召し上がりますか。	No, thank you. I'm full. 結構です。おなかがいっぱいです。

ファストフード店での表現

店員	客
For here or to go? こちらでお召し上がりですか。お持ち帰りですか。	To go. Can I get a hamburger and a coffee? 持ち帰りで。ハンバーガー1つとコーヒーを1ついただけますか。
Which size would you like, small, medium or large? S, M, Lのどちらのサイズにしますか。	Small one, please. Sをください。

練習問題

答えは別冊 P9

次の **(1)** から **(5)** までの会話について，(　　　) に入れるのに最も適切なものを **1**,**2**,**3**,**4** の中から一つ選びなさい。

(1) *Waiter:* (　　　)
Woman: Yes. I'll have egg sandwiches and coffee, please.
Waiter: OK. I'll be right back.

1 Can I change your order?
2 Are you ready to order?
3 Could I see the menu?
4 What's the special menu for today?

①②③④

(2) *Girl:* I'd like some tea, please.
Waiter: Certainly. (　　　)
Girl: No. That's all.

1 How many do you want?
2 What would you like to drink?
3 Anything else?
4 Sorry, but we don't have enough.

①②③④

(3) *Girl:* It's a beautiful place, Ms. Smith.
Woman: Welcome to our home, Lucy. (　　　)
Girl: Thank you so much.

1 Please help yourself to a drink.
2 Have a nice trip.
3 Thank you for inviting me.
4 I'd like something to drink.

①②③④

(4) *Boy:* Mom, I want to have curry for dinner. It's my favorite.
Mother: OK. Then I have no meat. (　　　)
Boy: Sorry, I have to do my homework now.

1 What do you want to have for lunch?
2 What do we need to make it?
3 Can you tell me how to make it?
4 Can you go to the supermarket now?

①②③④

(5) *Mother:* Would you like some more cookies, Mary?
Girl: No, thank you, Mom. (　　　)

1 I can't wait.　　**2** I'm full.
3 Same to you.　　**4** Are you all right?

①②③④

PART 19

会話表現⑤

道案内の会話

学習日

★理解度
□カンペキ!
□もう一度
□まだまだ…

３級では，目的地までの交通手段や道順を尋ねる表現が多く出題されます。答え方とあわせて覚えましょう。

迷ってしまったとき

I think we are lost.
私たちは迷ってしまったようです。

Let's ask someone.
だれかに聞こう。

声をかけるとき

(　　　　) me.
すみません。

I'll (　　　　) you the way.
私が行き方を教えましょう。

道を尋ねる＆教える表現

尋ねる	教える
Could you tell me (　　　　) to get to the Ueno station? 上野駅にはどうやって行けばいいか教えていただけますか。	Take the Yamanote Line at the Shinagawa station. 品川駅で山手線に乗ってください。
(　　　　) is Shinagawa Station? 品川駅はどこですか。	Go down this street. You'll get there in five minutes. この道を進んでください。5分で着きます。

練習問題

答えは別冊P10

次の (1) から (5) までの会話について，(　　) に入れるのに最も適切なものを1,2,3,4の中から一つ選びなさい。

(1) *Boy:* Is there a drugstore near here?
Girl: Yes. If you go straight, (　　)
1 I'll be there soon. **2** you'll find it on your left.
3 you should go back. **4** I'm going to the post office.
①②③④

(2) *Boy:* Excuse me. (　　)
Girl: Sure. Turn right at the second traffic light. Then you can see it right in front of you.
1 Could you tell me the way to the station?
2 I don't know when the train will come.
3 Please tell me where you are now.
4 Do you know the name of this building?
①②③④

(3) *Boy:* The hospital is not so far. You can go on foot.
Girl: (　　)
Boy: About ten minutes.
1 How can I get there? **2** Which bus should I take?
3 Why don't you take a taxi? **4** How long does it take?
①②③④

(4) *Boy:* Does this train go to Ikebukuro Station?
Girl: No. (　　) Take the Yamanote Line going toward Ikebukuro.
1 Change trains at the next stop.
2 You have to come to Ikebukuro.
3 How many stops are there?
4 You don't have to get off this train.
①②③④

(5) *Boy:* Excuse me. Is there a post office near here?
Girl: I'm sorry, but I don't know. (　　)
1 I'm a stranger here. **2** There isn't a bank around here.
3 What should I buy? **4** Where are you from?
①②③④

PART 20

長文A

掲示・案内①

学習日 

★理解度
□カンペキ！
□もう一度
□まだまだ…

３級で出題される長文は「掲示・案内」「メール」「説明文」の３種類です。まずは「掲示・案内」という短いお知らせ文を読んでいきましょう。

先に設問を読もう いきなり長文を読み始めるのではなく，まずは設問を読み長文の内容をつかみましょう。

設問1 What is the event held for?
(　　　　)は何のために(　　　　)のですか。

選択肢
1 Throwing away bad tomatoes.
悪くなったトマトを投げ捨てるため。
2 Volunteering for a fire department.
消防署のためにボランティアをするため。
3 Raising money for people in need.
困っている人々のために(　　　　)を集めるため。
4 Watching people in a fight.
戦っている人々を見るため。

解答(　　　　)

注意！
あてはまる日本語訳を考えて入れよう

設問2 People who take part in the event will
イベントに(　　　　)人は

選択肢
1 clean the streets after the fight.
戦いのあと，通りを掃除するでしょう。
2 send money to hungry people.
飢えた人々にお金を送るでしょう。
3 hit other people with tomatoes.
(　　　　)を他の人にぶつけるでしょう。
4 collect tomatoes from farms.
農場からトマトを集めるでしょう。

解答(　　　　)

注意！
右ページの長文を読んで，設問に対する答えを4つの選択肢から選ぼう

答えは別冊P 11

長文を読んでみよう　設問をふまえて，お知らせ文を読んでいきましょう。

Tomato Fight Against Hunger

Are you hoping to throw your worries away? Join the 15th annual Tomato-Throwing event! We have 6,000 pounds of tomatoes that are too bad to eat. Why don't you throw them at each other? You must feel like your stress goes away.

Date: Saturday, September 7th
Time: 3:30 p.m. to 4:30 p.m.
Place: East Side Fire Department

After the fight, the fire department will wash you off with a hose. Tickets are ten dollars. All the money you pay goes toward programs to help feed hungry people around the world.

Not brave enough to join the fight? Don't worry. You can just enjoy watching and donate.

For more information about the event, visit our website:
www.tomato-fight.com

練習問題

答えは別冊P11

次の掲示の内容に関して，*(1)*と *(2)* の質問に対する答えとして最も適切なもの，または文を完成させるのに最も適切なものを**1**,**2**,**3**,**4**の中から一つ選びなさい。

World Cup Watching Tour

The 9th FIFA Women's World Cup will be held from July 10 to August 20, 2023, in Australia and New Zealand. Thirty-two teams will play to win the cup. The United States team, the 8th tournament champion, will join the games to keep their title.
Here's your chance not only to watch the exciting games at excellent seats, but also to enjoy sightseeing in the beautiful countries.

Packages :
Luxury: Australia only
Luxury: New Zealand only
Luxury: Both Countries
Economy: Australia only

All packages include plane tickets, hotel coupons with breakfast, land transportation, and the game tickets. Luxury packages include 3 dinners with players and coaches.

For package details and prices, contact Christine at FIFA Travel USA 1-887-863-9681.

(1) Where will the games be played?

1 In Australia.

2 In New Zealand.

3 In the United States.

4 In New Zealand and Australia.

1 2 3 4

(2) Those who choose the economy package will miss

1 traveling by plane.

2 having meals with guests.

3 getting into games.

4 having breakfast in the hotel.

1 2 3 4

PART 21

長文A

掲示・案内②

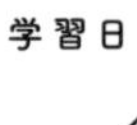

学習日

★理解度
□カンペキ！
□もう一度
□まだまだ…

「掲示・案内」という短いお知らせ文を読んでいきましょう。

先に設問を読もう いきなり長文を読み始めるのではなく，まずは設問を読み長文の内容をつかみましょう。

設問1 When will the language exams be held?

語学の試験は（　　　　　）行われますか。

選択肢

1 On Tuesday, June 8.
6月8日火曜日。

2 On Wednesday, June 9.
6月9日水曜日。

3 On Thursday June 10.
6月10日（　　　　　）。

4 On Friday, June 11.
6月11日金曜日。

解答（　　　　　）

設問2 The exams in the other subjects will take place

他の教科の試験が行われるのは

選択肢

1 after economics exams are completed.
経済の試験が終わったあと。

2 in the cafeteria.
（　　　　　）で。

3 in the meeting room.
会議室で。

4 before Friday, June 4.
6月4日金曜日以前。

解答（　　　　　）

覚えよう
設問の続きを選ぶ問題もあります

答えは別冊P12

長文を読んでみよう　設問をふまえて，お知らせ文を読んでいきましょう。

Year End Examination Schedule

Your teachers have decided the schedule of this year's final examinations. Each date has each subject area, so students just have to take an exam a day from each area.

Date	Subject(s)
Tuesday, June 8	Science
Wednesday, June 9	Mathematics
Thursday, June 10	English, Spanish, French, German
Friday, June 11	History, Government, Economics
Examinations in other subjects will be held on Monday, June 7.	

All exams for all students will be held in the cafeteria.
You cannot use the cafeteria during the exam period, so the meeting room will be open instead.

If you have questions about examinations, be sure to ask your teacher before Friday, June 4.

練習問題

答えは別冊P12

次の掲示の内容に関して，*(1)*と *(2)* の質問に対する答えとして最も適切なもの，または文を完成させるのに最も適切なものを**1**,**2**,**3**,**4**の中から一つ選びなさい。

Millennium African Festival

It's that season again! Join people who love African music and culture. This year, there will be lots of special programs to celebrate the festival's 20th birthday. Don't miss them!

Dates: August 20, 21 and 22
Time: 10 a.m. until midnight
Place: Millennium Park
Events:
- Live performances (African music & dance on stage)
- African drums lessons for adults and children
- Guest Talk (about history and culture of African countries)
- African Market (African food, drink and products)

Tickets: $15 per day; $5 for children under 8

For more information about the festival, visit our website:
www.millenniumafricanfest.com

(1) How much will it cost for a mother, father and 2 children under 8 to attend the festival?

1 $20.

2 $40.

3 $45.

4 $100.

(2) People attending the festival won't be able to

1 listen to performances of African music.

2 enjoy watching African dancing.

3 learn to speak African languages.

4 try African dishes.

PART 22

長文B

メール①

学習日

★理解度
□カンペキ！
□もう一度
□まだまだ…

続いて「メール」文を読んでいきましょう。メールは1往復のものと1往復半のものがあります。

覚えよう

From：送信者
To：受信者
Date：日付
Subject：件名
はメールの最初につきます

先に設問を読もう いきなり長文を読み始めるのではなく，まずは設問を読み長文の内容をつかみましょう。

設問1 Why is Yuina nervous?

ユイナは（　　　　　）緊張しているのですか。

選択肢
1 She cannot speak English at all.
2 She has to perform on the stage.
3 She has never been outside of Japan.
4 She is not good at swimming.

解答（　　　　　）

設問2 Yuina started to study English

ユイナが英語を（　　　　　）し始めたのは

選択肢
1 at school.
2 to watch musicals.
3 to travel abroad.
4 five years ago.

解答（　　　　　）

設問3 What plan has Daisy's family made?

デイジーの家族は何の（　　　　　）を立てましたか。

選択肢
1 Take Yuina to the sea.
2 Give Yuina English lessons.
3 Hold a big festival.
4 Buy a new jacket.

解答（　　　　　）

答えは別冊P13

長文を読んでみよう　設問をふまえて，メール文を読んでいきましょう。

From: Yuina Tanaka
To: Daisy Neuman
Date: June 14
Subject: Hello from Japan!

Dear Daisy,
Hi! I am Yuina. I will be staying at your home for two weeks in July. I am glad that you and your parents will be my host family. I am so excited to get a chance to study in Canada. This is my first time to travel abroad, so I am a little nervous. I have studied English for five years, but I am still not good at speaking. I hope you will understand my English. I'm in the drama club at school. My dream is to be an actor in musicals and perform on international stages. For that reason, I want to be better at English. I also hope I can make many memories with you. I'm looking forward to meeting you soon.
Sincerely,
Yuina

From: Daisy Neuman
To: Yuina Tanaka
Date: June 14
Subject: I can't wait!

Hi Yuina,
Please don't be nervous. We're going to have a wonderful time together. I have no brothers or sisters, so I'm happy to be your host sister. It is great of you to have a clear goal and try your best. I hope your dream will come true. Actually, our city is perfect for you! A big festival to enjoy performing arts is held here during your stay. Many people around the world come and see the shows every year. I'm sure you will have fun! The temperature of the night and day is so different here, so you need a jacket. Also, don't forget to bring a swimming suit. We are planning to take you to the sea. Send me all of your questions.
Your new sister,
Daisy

練習問題

答えは別冊P13

次のEメールの内容に関して, *(1)* から *(3)* までの質問に対する答えとして最も適切なものを**1**,**2**,**3**,**4**の中から一つ選びなさい。

From: Linda McDonald
To: Carolyn McDonald
Date: October 27
Subject: Are you interested?

Good morning!
Do you have breakfast every day? You know breakfast is important. These days, your dad and I drink fresh milk every morning. There is a company which delivers milk to each home. The company has their own farm and gives their cows high-quality food, so their milk is safe and healthy. Also, it's eco-friendly because it comes in glass bottles that are returned and reused. They deliver twice a week. It's more expensive than milk from the supermarket, but much tastier! Would you like to try a bottle?
Love,
Mom

From: Carolyn McDonald
To: Linda McDonald
Date: October 28
Subject: How about this?

Hi Mom,
That sounds interesting! I visited their website to know more about it. Other than milk, we can order ice cream, butter, yogurt and three types of cheese. I want to try their ice cream, but there are some problems. I'm usually not at home during the daytime, and the mailbox is not a good place to keep ice cream and others. So I have an idea. I'll ask them to deliver my orders to your house. Can I ask you to keep mine cold together with your orders? I'll stop by on my way home from work twice a week and take my orders home. I think it is also good for us to sometimes have dinner together. What do you think?
Hugs,
Carolyn

(1) What is special about the milk?

1 Cheaper than the market price.

2 Good for the environment.

3 Easy to get.

4 Not necessary to be kept cold. ① ② ③ ④

(2) What food items cannot be ordered from the company?

1 Milk and cheese.

2 Yogurt and ice cream.

3 Meat and fish.

4 Butter and cheese. ① ② ③ ④

(3) Why does Carolyn want to have her orders delivered to Linda's house?

1 She is away when her orders arrive.

2 Her apartment building has no mailboxes.

3 The company doesn't deliver to Carolyn's area.

4 Linda's house is nearer to her office. ① ② ③ ④

PART 23 長文B
メール②

学習日

★理解度
□カンペキ！
□もう一度
□まだまだ…

「メール」文を読んでいきましょう。

先に設問を読もう いきなり長文を読み始めるのではなく，まずは設問を読み長文の内容をつかみましょう。

覚えよう

Subject（件名）は，メール文を読むためのヒントになります

設問1 What aren't the girls going to do at the party?

女の子たちは（　　　　　）で何をしないつもりですか。

選択肢
1 Eat lots of snacks.
2 Play video games.
3 Watch several movies.
4 Sleep for hours.

解答（　　　　　）

設問2 Amelia asks Erica to eat dinner with her family because

アメリアはエリカに自分の家族と一緒に（　　　　　）をとるように頼みました。なぜなら

選択肢
1 Erica needs to arrive early.
2 Erica has to go home by seven.
3 Erica doesn't like snacks.
4 They want to talk before the others arrive.

解答（　　　　　）

設問3 Why was Samantha invited?

サマンサはなぜ（　　　　　）されたのですか。

選択肢
1 She is in Erica's art class.
2 Her mother works at night.
3 She is going to invite Lizzy.
4 Lizzy wasn't able to come.

解答（　　　　　）

長文を読んでみよう 設問をふまえて，メール文を読んでいきましょう。

From: Amelia Jensen
To: Erica Gonzalez
Date: June 14
Subject: Party at my house

Hi Erica,
I'm so glad that school has ended! My parents say I can celebrate with a party because my grades were good. I can invite four girls to an all-night party. I think we will enjoy talking and listening to music, not sleeping. What do you think? The party would start at 7 in the evening and end at 10 in the morning. Which night would be better for you, next Friday or next Saturday? Please let me know.
Amelia

From: Erica Gonzalez
To: Amelia Jensen
Date: June 14
Subject: Sounds exciting!

Hi Amelia,
That's great! Either night will work for me. I'll bring my computer. I have lots of games we can play. Could I arrive at 6:30? My mom will drive me to your house. She has to be at work by 7 p.m. on weekends. Who else are you inviting?
Talk to you soon,
Erica

From: Amelia Jensen
To: Erica Gonzalez
Date: June 14
Subject: Party on Saturday

Hi Erica,
Of course, you can arrive at 6:30! Would you like to come earlier and eat dinner with me and my family? I was hoping Lizzy could come, but she's going to be out of town all weekend. I invited Samantha from our art class instead. The party is going to be on Saturday because that was the best for Carson, Julia and Samantha. They're bringing music and movies. My mother is making lots of snacks for the five of us. Let's have fun all night!
Your best friend,
Amelia

練習問題

答えは別冊P15

次のEメールの内容に関して, *(1)* から *(3)* までの質問に対する答えとして最も適切なものを**1**,**2**,**3**,**4**の中から一つ選びなさい。

From: Ryan Silver
To: Keita Harada
Date: March 30
Subject: How are you doing?

Hi Keita,
Two weeks have passed since you left my house. It was so much fun to have a Japanese brother. I understand you had to go back before the start of the Japanese school year, but I miss you! I'm sorry you will miss the end of the American school year in June. Thanks for giving me your *soroban*. I just love it. Can you tell me how to use it? You are so good at doing math in your head. I would like to be able to do that. Teach me your secrets!
Your friend,
Ryan

From: Keita Harada
To: Ryan Silver
Date: April 1
Subject: You are welcome

Hi Ryan,
I miss you too. I miss your family and all of my American friends. You were so kind to me during my stay in America. Now, I have some difficulties returning to my life in Japan. I sometimes forget I'm not in America anymore. Yesterday, I almost forgot to take off my shoes when I entered my house. I'm glad you like my *soroban*. Maybe you need some practice to use it very well. Japanese children learn how to use it at school. I'll email a file to you. It tells how you can use *soroban* to improve your mental math skills.
Your Japanese brother,
Keita

From: Ryan Silver
To: Keita Harada
Date: April 1
Subject: Wonderful!

Hi Keita,
Thank you for sending the file. Tim and Jenny, our friends from math class, are also interested in *soroban*. Now we're all trying to learn by reading your file. I think we will get better at using *soroban* little by little. I'll let you know how it goes again.
Thanks,
Ryan

(1) Why do Ryan and Keita know each other?

1 Keita stayed with Ryan's family.

2 Tim and Jenny introduced Ryan to Keita.

3 Ryan was an exchange student in Japan.

4 Keita was Ryan's math teacher.

① ② ③ ④

(2) What did Ryan need help with?

1 Using a Japanese tool for math.

2 Following the Japanese customs.

3 Learning to write Japanese characters.

4 Sending a file by email.

① ② ③ ④

(3) What are Ryan, Tim and Jenny doing together?

1 Taking a math examination.

2 Making math problems.

3 Learning to use *soroban*.

4 Teaching children in math class.

① ② ③ ④

PART 24

長文C

説明文①

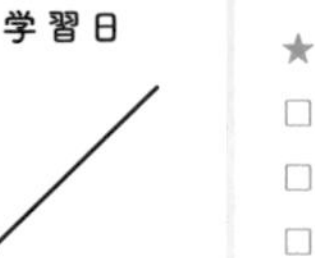

★理解度
□カンペキ!
□もう一度
□まだまだ…

先に設問を読もう 最後に「説明文」を読んでいきます。まずは設問を読み長文の内容をつかみましょう。

段落ごとに内容をつかもう

設問1 How were the Lascaux Cave paintings discovered?

ラスコー洞窟の壁画は，どのように(　　　　)されましたか。

選択肢
1 Dr. Rappenglueck was looking for old star maps.
2 Some people went into the cave for hunting.
3 A dog fell into a hole and its owner looked for him.
4 Four French teenagers went out for a walk.

解答 (　　　　)

設問2 When were the drawings made?

壁画は(　　　　)作られましたか。

選択肢
1 At least 15,000 years ago.
2 In 1963.
3 More than 17,000 years ago.
4 Less than eighty years ago.

解答 (　　　　)

設問3 What happened in 1963?

1963年に(　　　　)が起きましたか。

選択肢
1 A cave with paintings was opened to visitors.
2 A German scientist found the oldest star map in the cave.
3 Damage to the paintings led to closing the cave to visitors.
4 Four boys happened to find old paintings in a cave.

解答 (　　　　)

設問4 What is this story about?

この話は何についてですか。

長文のタイトルもヒントになります

選択肢
1 The adventures of Marcel and his dog Robot.
2 A cave with very old paintings studied by scientists.
3 How maps in a cave were saved.
4 The danger to teenagers going into caves.

解答 (　　　　)

長文を読んでみよう　設問をふまえて，説明文を読んでいきましょう。

Oldest Map of the Stars

More than eighty years ago, Marcel, a French teenager, went out for a walk with his dog, Robot. Suddenly the dog fell through a small hole in the ground. Marcel ran to get three friends and some candles, and the boys went to look for Robot. What they found were hundreds of drawings of animals on walls in a cave*– and Robot.

Scientists who studied the drawings found that they were made between 15,000 to 17,000 years ago. There were very fine paintings of horses, deer, cats and other animals. Some of them are now extinct or imaginary. You can also see a man with the head of a bird. They believed the cave was used for a very long time for ceremonies to pray for successful hunting.

The Lascaux Cave and its wonderful paintings soon became famous, and many people came to see them. The drawings were touched by too many visitors and their state soon became worse. CO_2 in visitors' breath also damaged the drawings. In 1963 the cave was closed. Only a few scientists every year can enter it.

One of those scientists, a German named Dr. Rappenglueck, now believes that a few of the drawings are the oldest maps of the stars. He thinks one map shows where the stars Vega, Deneb and Altair were 16,500 years ago. Another drawing may stand for a map of the Pleiades star cluster* as it was long ago. You can't visit the Lascaux Cave paintings that Marcel discovered, but in a nearby cave there are copies of the drawings. Thousands of visitors go to see them every year. Maybe someday you will go there too.

*cave：洞窟　　*the Pleiades star cluster：プレアデス星団

練習問題

答えは別冊 P 17

次の英文の内容に関して，*(1)* から *(5)* までの質問に対する答えとして最も適切なもの，または文を完成させるのに最も適切なものを**1**,**2**,**3**,**4**の中から一つ選びなさい。

A Plan for Clean Energy

Climate change is one of the biggest problems we have. Scientists have been worried about it for a long time. Because of climate change, there are bigger storms, huge forest fires and floods all over the world. Scientists think growing CO_2 emissions* causes climate change. Global CO_2 emissions are largely from fossil fuels.* Now we should think about using clean energy. One example is solar power.*

The U.S. Department of Energy* (DOE) recently talked about plans to stop using fossil fuels. The U.S. plans to use 100% clean electricity* by 2035. Solar power is an important part of that plan. They want to produce solar power at lower cost. Their goal is to cut the cost of solar power by 60% in the next ten years.

To reach the goal, DOE will spend over $128 million. They think it is necessary to improve solar power technologies. They are also paying for better electricity factories and better ways to deliver the power.

On the other hand, some people do not like the plan. Some say that the goal is too difficult to be reached so quickly. Others say that the plan needs too much money and the cost will be shared with users. In their opinion, people will continue to pay more for solar electricity. And some people still feel fossil fuels will always be necessary. DOE says that strong goals and money to reach them are necessary for success.

*CO_2 emission：二酸化炭素排出量
*fossil fuel：化石燃料
*solar power：太陽光発電
*Department of Energy：エネルギー省
*electricity：電気

(1) What have scientists been worried about?

1 Huge forest fires.

2 Floods.

3 Climate change.

4 Ocean temperatures.

①②③④

(2) The goal of the U.S. Department of Energy

1 is to cut the cost of solar electricity by 60%.

2 was to spend over $128 million.

3 is to make fossil fuels better.

4 is to stop huge forest fires.

①②③④

(3) When does the United States plan to use only clean electricity?

1 Before 2020.

2 By 2035.

3 After 2030.

4 By 2025.

①②③④

(4) Some people don't agree to the DOE's plans because

1 climate change is not a big problem.

2 the period of ten years is too long.

3 there is another clean energy.

4 it is not so easy to realize the plan.

①②③④

(5) What is this story about?

1 Department of Energy pollution.

2 Making solar electricity cheaper.

3 Problems of climate change.

4 Rising cost of electricity.

①②③④

PART 25

長文C

説明文②

★理解度
□カンペキ!
□もう一度
□まだまだ…

先に設問を読もう 「説明文」を読んでいきます。まずは設問を読み長文の内容をつかみましょう。

設問1 March Madness
マーチマッドネスは

選択肢
1 takes place once every four years.
2 is the best basketball team in the U.S.
3 is a university sports tournament.
4 starts on the first Sunday in March.

解答（　　　）

設問2 March Madness is popular because
マーチマッドネスは（　　　）があります。なぜなら

選択肢
1 the games are usually very exciting.
2 basketball players are so tall.
3 so many people go to the games.
4 the games are held in universities.

解答（　　　）

設問3 People can take part in the Bracket Challenge by
人々が勝ち上がり予想に（　　　）することができるのは

選択肢
1 playing university basketball.
2 paying a small amount of money.
3 listening to a committee.
4 writing the names of winning teams.

解答（　　　）

設問4 Why is it difficult to win the Bracket Challenge?
勝ち上がり予想に勝つのが（　　　）のはなぜですか。

選択肢
1 Basketball tournaments are difficult to win.
2 Too many people join the game each year.
3 There are too many possible answers.
4 The game is controlled by the committee.

解答（　　　）

覚えよう

段落ごとのまとまりで内容を整理しながら読みます

答えは別冊P18

長文を読んでみよう　設問をふまえて，説明文を読んでいきましょう。

March Madness

During the month of March, many people all over the U.S. are excited about a sports tournament. It decides the number one men's university basketball team in the United States. The best 68 teams play against each other. Most Americans talk about these games, even if they don't watch. The tournament is called "March Madness."

March Madness is so popular. One of the reasons is the games themselves are usually very exciting. It's common for many of them to go into overtime*. Sometimes one excellent shot* turns a game around in the last 10 seconds.

Another reason is you can enjoy expecting which team will win. It's the *March Madness Bracket* Challenge Game*. Everyone can join it, even if they are not basketball fans. On a Sunday in the middle of March, a committee* tells which 68 teams can join the tournament. On that same day, the committee gives out online "brackets." You guess which team will win each game in the tournament and write their names in the bracket. You can take part in the game for free, and the winner receives $1 million.

Unfortunately, no one has ever got the prize money. Why? Because there are many games in the tournament and it's almost impossible to guess right about all the games. Also, they are full of more drama than anyone can imagine. That's why people are crazy about March Madness.

*overtime：試合延長時間　*shot：シュート　*bracket：トーナメント表　*committee：委員会

練習問題

答えは別冊P18

次の英文の内容に関して，*(1)* から *(5)* までの質問に対する答えとして最も適切なもの，または文を完成させるのに最も適切なものを**1**,**2**,**3**,**4**の中から一つ選びなさい。

Cherry Blossom Season in America

In Japan, Yukio Ozaki is known as "the father of the Japanese Constitution,*" but in the United States he is famous for another reason. When he was mayor of Tokyo City, Ozaki sent 3,000 Japanese Yoshino cherry trees to the U.S. as a symbol of friendship between the two countries. The trees were planted along the Potmac River in Washington D.C. in 1912, and loved by many people.

Every spring, the National Cherry Blossom Festival* is held there for about three weeks in March and April. The festival started in 1927. Now, more than 1.5 million people from all over the world come to see the beautiful cherry blossoms every year.

About 50 of the 3,000 first trees are still alive. They are 109 years old, but still show their beautiful blossoms in spring. It's rare for Yoshino cherry trees to live more than 50 years. These trees are taken good care of. When one of them dies, a new tree takes over. It is often planted by a First Lady, the wife of an American president. For example, Michelle Obama planted one in 2012.

While the one in Washington D.C. is the most famous, other places in the United States also celebrate their own cherry blossom season. For example, people come to Door County, Wisconsin, in the middle of the country, to see thousands of cherry trees. Their blossom season comes in mid-May. In Portland, Oregon, close to the Pacific Ocean, there is a Japanese American Historical Plaza which has 100 Akebono cherry trees. People enjoy their blossoms usually in mid-March.

*constitution：立憲政治　　*the National Cherry Blossom Festival：全米桜祭り

(1) Why is Yukio Ozaki famous in America?

1 He helped build the government.
2 He was kind to the wife of an American president.
3 For the gift he gave to America.
4 For starting the first American Cherry Blossom Festival.

① ② ③ ④

(2) The National Cherry Blossom Festival

1 started in 1912.
2 is held in mid-May.
3 lasts for a week.
4 takes place in Washington D.C.

① ② ③ ④

(3) Yoshino cherry trees usually live

1 for less than 50 years.
2 until they stop producing flowers.
3 for over 100 years.
4 until they are pulled out.

① ② ③ ④

(4) In which of the four cities does cherry blossom season come last in the year?

1 Tokyo.
2 Washington D.C.
3 Door County.
4 Portland.

① ② ③ ④

(5) What is this story about?

1 The people who plant cherry trees.
2 How much cherry blossoms are loved in America.
3 How long cherry trees can live.
4 Friendship between the people of Japan and America.

① ② ③ ④

PART 26

英作文①Eメール
形式の注意点

学習日

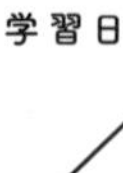

★理解度
□カンペキ!
□もう一度
□まだまだ…

ライティング（英作文）では「Eメール」を書く問題が出題されます。

①注意!
内容・語彙・文法の3つの観点で採点されます。各観点4点で，12点満点です。
なお，カンマ（,）やピリオド（.）は語数には含めません

ルールを押さえよう

「Eメール」の問題でのルールを確認しましょう。

・「2つの質問」に答えること　・「15~25語で」書くこと
・相手のEメールに対応した内容であること

質問に使われる表現

Eメールに書かれた質問の内容を理解するために，質問でよく使われる表現を確認しましょう。

「何？」 (　　　　) kind of food do you like?（あなたが好きな食べ物の種類は何ですか）
「だれ？」 (　　　　) do you respect?（あなたはだれを尊敬していますか）
「どこ？」 (　　　　) did you go last winter?（あなたはこの前の冬にどこに行きましたか）
「どのような？」 (　　　　) was your vacation?（あなたの休暇はどうでしたか）
「いくつ？」 How (　　　　) classes were there?（クラスの数はいくつでしたか）

「いつ~?」	When ~?	「なぜ~?」	Why ~?	「どっち~?」	Which ~?

質問への返答に使える表現

質問に対する返答を書く際に使える表現を確認しましょう。

I like ~	私は~〈物など〉が好きです	I 　　　 to ~	私は~〈場所〉へ行きました
I 　　　 ~	私は~〈人物〉を尊敬しています	It's 　　　 ~	~〈理由〉だからです
My birthday is ~	私の誕生日は~〈時〉です	It was ~	~〈様子〉でした

冒頭文を書く

返信メールでは，いきなり質問に答えるのではなく，まずは相手のEメールの内容に対応した冒頭文を書きましょう。

That's wonderful!（それはすてきですね）
I'm (　　　　) hard every day.（私は毎日一生懸命に勉強をしています）
I (　　　　) a great summer vacation.（私の夏休みはすばらしかったです）

締めくくりの文を書く

最後に，締めくくりの文を書きましょう。

覚えよう
語数調整をしながら文をふくらませましょう

I'm really excited about the trip.（私は旅行が本当に楽しみです）
I will do my (　　　　) for the test.（私はテストのためにベストを尽くします）
I hope to see you (　　　　).（いつかあなたに会えることを願っています）

練習問題

答えは別冊 P 20

次の（　　）に入れるのに適切な語を，《　　》から選んで書き入れましょう。

- あなたは，外国人の友達（Laurie）から以下のEメールを受け取りました。Eメールを読み，それに対する返信メールを，[　　]に英文で書きなさい。
- あなたが書く返信メールの中で，友達（Laurie）からの2つの質問（下線部）に対応する内容を，あなた自身で自由に考えて答えなさい。
- あなたが書く返信メールの中で[　　]に書く英文の語数の目安は，15語～25語です。

> Hi,
>
> How are you doing?
> You told me that you are going on vacation next week. I went to Hawaii with my family last weekend. Where will you go? Also, what will you do there? Please tell me about it!
>
> Your friend,
> Laurie

質問の内容の確認

Where will you go?　→「どこ？」と，行く場所を尋ねています。

あなたはどこへ行きますか。

Also, what will you do there?　→「何？」と，何をするのか尋ねています。

それと，そこで何をしますか。

返信メール

> Hi, Laurie!
>
> Thank you for your e-mail.
>
> Did you enjoy (　　　　)? I'll (　　　　) to Yamanashi (　　　　) week. I'll (　　　　) the beautiful (　　　　) of Mt. Fuji! I have (　　　　) been there before.
>
> Best wishes,

《 enjoy　go　next　Hawaii　never　view 》

PART 27

英作文②Eメール
実践

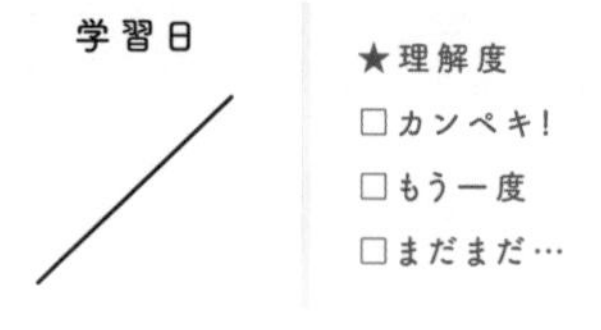

本番の形式に近い形でEメールの返信を書いてみましょう。

> Hello,
>
> Thanks for writing me.
> You wrote that you went camping last weekend. I want to hear all about it! Who did you go with? How was the weather? I'm going camping soon, too.
>
> Your friend,
> Mark

冒頭文を書こう
まずは，Eメールの内容を受けた冒頭文を書きましょう。

You wrote that you went camping last weekend.に対して
あなたは先週末キャンプに行ったと書いていました

はい，その通りです。	はい，私はキャンプに行きました。
Yes, (　　　　　) right.	Yes, I (　　　　　) camping.

I'm going camping soon, too.に対して
私も近々，キャンプに行きます

わあ，それはすばらしいですね。
Oh, (　　　　　) great.

2つの質問に答えよう
質問の内容を確認し，それに対する答えを書きましょう。

Who did you go with? あなたはだれと行きましたか

私は家族とキャンプに行きました。
I went camping (　　　　　) my (　　　　　).

How was the weather? 天気はどうでしたか

晴れて暖かかったです。
(　　　　　) was (　　　　　) and warm.

締めくくりの文を書く
最後に締めくくりの文を書きましょう。

また行けるといいと思います。	次は一緒に行きましょう。
I (　　　　　) we can go again.	(　　　　　) go together next time.

練習問題

答えは別冊P21

- あなたは，外国人の友達（Josh）から以下のEメールを受け取りました。Eメールを読み，それに対する返信メールを，[　　　]に英文で書きなさい。
- あなたが書く返信メールの中で，友達（Josh）からの2つの質問（下線部）に対応する内容を，あなた自身で自由に考えて答えなさい。
- あなたが書く返信メールの中で[　　　]に書く英文の語数の目安は，15語～25語です。

Hi,

I went to your house today, but you weren't at home. Where did you go? Also, what did you do there? I am free all weekend. Let's do something together tomorrow!

Your friend,
Josh

Hi, Josh!

Thank you for your e-mail.

[　　　　　　　　　　]

Kind regards,

PART 28

英作文③意見論述

形式の注意点

学習日

★理解度
□カンペキ!
□もう一度
□まだまだ…

ライティング２問目では，「外国人の友達から質問された」という設定でQUESTIONが出題されます。

ルールを押さえよう

意見論述の問題では，守らないと減点になったり，採点の対象外になったりするルールがあります。

- 「意見とその理由を２つ」書くこと
- 「25~35語で」書くこと
- QUESTIONに対応した内容であること

注意!

カンマ(,)やピリオド(.)は語数には含めません

解答文の基本の構成を理解しよう

解答文を書くとき，書き方のフォーマットを知っていると便利です。

賛成・反対の表明	賛成の場合　I think that ~（~と思います） 反対の場合　I don't think ~（~とは思いません）
理由①	First, ~（第一に，~）
理由②	Second, ~（第二に，~）

覚えよう

さまざまな表現を覚えておくと，語数の調整にも使えます

使える表現

他にも使える表現を覚えておきましょう。

I think (that) ~	~と思います	I agree (that) ~	~ということに賛成です
I don't ＿＿ (that) ~	~とは思いません	I don't ＿＿ (that) ~	~ということには賛成しません
I disagree (that) ~	~ということには反対です	My favorite ~ is ...	私が大好きな~は…です

first	第一に	first of all	まず第一に
second	第二に	also	また
for example	＿＿	such as	~のような
in addition	さらには	moreover	そのうえ
not only that	それだけでなく	on the other hand	その一方で
in spite of that	それにもかかわらず	because of this	このため
in my opinion	私の＿＿では	for these reasons	これらの＿＿により
therefore	したがって	that's why ~	それが~の理由です

練習問題

答えは別冊 P 22

次の（　　　）に入れるのに適切な語句を，[　　　] から選んで書き入れましょう。ただし先頭にくる語も小文字になっています。

- あなたは，外国人の友達から以下の**QUESTION**をされました。
- **QUESTION**について，あなたの意見とその理由を2つ英文で書きなさい。
- 語数の目安は25語〜35語です。

QUESTION: ***Which do you like better, dogs or cats?***

質問：あなたは犬と猫のどちらがより好きですか。

犬のほうが好きな場合

I (　　　　) dogs better. I (　　　　) two (　　　　). (　　　　), dogs are smart, so some dogs work for the police. (　　　　), I can walk and play outside with them. It is good for my health.

first	like	reasons	second	have

猫のほうが好きな場合

I (　　　　) cats better. I (　　　　　　　　). (　　　　), cats don't bark loudly, (　　　　) they aren't noisy in my room. (　　　　), I don't have to take them for a walk. Keeping them isn't hard.

first	like	so	second	have two reasons

PART 29

英作文④意見論述

ブレインストーミング

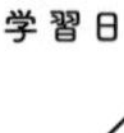
学習日

★理解度
□カンペキ!
□もう一度
□まだまだ…

意見論述の問題では，いきなり答えを書き始めるのではなく，質問を見て答えの候補を挙げていくと書きやすくなります。

QUESTION : ***What subject do you like studying the best?***
質問：あなたはどの教科を勉強することが一番好きですか。

理科が好きな場合

I like studying science the best.
私は理科を勉強することが一番好きです。

その理由をいくつか挙げよう

・動物や植物について学ぶことが好き。
I like learning () animals and plants.

・理科の授業は楽しい。
() classes are fun.

・理科は日常生活に役立つ。
Science is ( ) for everyday life.

・将来エンジニアになりたいので，もっと理科を勉強したい。
I want to be an ( ) in the future, so I want to study science more.

注意!

理由は，まったく違うことについて書きます。同じような内容だと減点されてしまいます

英語が好きな場合

I like studying English the best.
私は英語を勉強することが一番好きです。

その理由をいくつか挙げよう

・英語で映画を楽しみたい。
I want to ( ) many movies in English.

・外国の友達を作りたい。
I want to make a lot of friends from ( ) countries.

・さまざまな文化を学ぶことは興味深い。
Learning different cultures is ( ).

・海外旅行で役に立つ。
English is useful when I ( ) abroad.

練習問題

答えは別冊P22

QUESTION: ***Which do you like better, eating out or at home?***

質問：外食と家で食べるのでは，どちらが好きですか。

上の質問について，好きな理由を日本語でそれぞれ４つずつ書きましょう。できるだけ簡単な日本語で書くのがコツです。

外食が好きな場合

- (例)家族以外の人との食事を楽しめる。
-
-
-
-

家で食べるのが好きな場合

- (例)時間を気にしなくてよい。
-
-
-
-

上で書いた理由のうち，英語にできそうなものをそれぞれ２つずつ選び，英語で書きましょう。

外食が好きな場合

-
-

家で食べるのが好きな場合

-
-

PART 30

英作文⑤意見論述

和文英訳

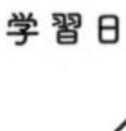

学習日　　／

★理解度
□カンペキ！
□もう一度
□まだまだ…

本番の形式に近い形で練習していきましょう。

QUESTION：***Do you often go to the library?***

質問：あなたは（　　　　　　）によく行きますか。

上の質問について，あなたの意見とその理由２つを日本語で書きましょう。

はい・いいえ
私は図書館に（　　　　　　　　　　　　　　　　）。
理由は２つあります。
１つ目は（
　　　　　　　　　　　　　　　　　　　　　　）からです。
２つ目は（
　　　　　　　　　　　　　　　　　　　　　　）からです。

上で書いた日本語を英訳しましょう。

覚えよう

Do you ～?には
YesやNoで答えます

注意！

英訳しやすいように，
かんたんな日本語で
書くのがコツです

練習問題

答えは別冊 P 23

- あなたは，外国人の友達から以下の**QUESTION**をされました。
- **QUESTION**について，あなたの意見とその理由を2つ英文で書きなさい。
- 語数の目安は25語～35語です。

QUESTION : ***What country do you want to visit?***

PART 31

リスニング第1部

会話の続きを選ぶ①

学習日

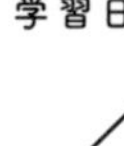

★理解度
□カンペキ!
□もう一度
□まだまだ…

リスニングには，第１部・第２部・第３部があります。第１部は，イラストを見ながら２人の会話を聞き，最後の応答を選ぶ問題です。

状況を把握しよう 放送を聞く前に，問題用紙に印刷されているイラストを見て，どんな状況なのかを把握しておきましょう。

注意!

問題用紙にはイラストしか印刷されていません

考えてみよう イラストを見て，わかることに丸を付けましょう。

①女性の職業は？　銀行員 ・ 医師 ・ 司書

②男性は何をしようとしている？　口座を開く ・ 診察を受ける ・ 本を借りる

TR 01

音声を聞いて，問題を解いてみよう 解答 (　　　　)

読まれた英文 もう一度音声を聞き，空欄をうめましょう。

A: Hi.

B: Hello. (　　　　) I borrow this book, please?

A: Of course, you can. (　　　　) you have a library card?

1 I haven't read it.

2 (　　　　), here you are.

3 For two weeks.

注意!

会話の最後の文をしっかり聞き取ろう

日本語訳

A: こんにちは。

B: こんにちは。この本を借りてもいいですか。

A: もちろんいいですよ。図書館のカードを持っていますか。

1 それを読んでいません。

2 はい，どうぞ。

3 2週間です。

練習問題  TR 02

答えは別冊P24

イラストを参考にしながら対話と応答を聞き，最も適切な応答を**1**,**2**,**3**の中から一つ選びなさい。

(1)

1 2 3

(2)

1 2 3

(3)

1 2 3

(4)

1 2 3

(5)

1 2 3

(6)

1 2 3

PART 32

リスニング第1部

会話の続きを選ぶ②

学習日

★理解度
□カンペキ!
□もう一度
□まだまだ…

第1部は，イラストを見ながら2人の会話を聞き，最後の応答を選ぶ問題です。問題用紙にはイラストしか印刷されていません。

状況を把握しよう 放送を聞く前に，問題用紙に印刷されているイラストを見て，どんな状況なのかを把握しておきましょう。

考えてみよう イラストを見て，わかることに丸を付けましょう。

①場所はどこ？ 部屋の中 ・ 学校の教室 ・ レストラン

②女性は何をしようとしている？

買い物をする ・ 授業を受ける ・ 机を持ち上げる

覚えよう

イラストの状況をイメージしながら音声を聞こう

TR 03

音声を聞いて，問題を解いてみよう 解答（　　　）

読まれた英文 もう一度音声を聞き，空欄をうめましょう。

A: Do you need any help?

B: Yes, please. This desk is too (　　　) for me.

A: No problem. (　　　) do you want to move it?

1 Over there (　　　) the window.

2 Sorry, I'm busy now.

3 Thanks for helping me.

日本語訳

A: 手伝おうか。

B: ええ，お願い。この机は私には重すぎるの。

A: 問題ないよ。どこへ動かしたいの？

1 向こうの窓のそばに。

2 ごめんなさい，今は忙しいの。

3 手伝ってくれてありがとう。

練習問題  TR 04

答えは別冊P25

イラストを参考にしながら対話と応答を聞き，最も適切な応答を**1**,**2**,**3**の中から一つ選びなさい。

(1)

① ② ③

(2)

① ② ③

(3)

① ② ③

(4)

① ② ③

(5)

① ② ③

(6)

① ② ③

PART 33

リスニング第2部

会話の内容を聞き取る①

学習日

★理解度
□カンペキ!
□もう一度
□まだまだ…

続いて，第２部を練習していきましょう。第２部では，２人の会話と，その会話の内容についての質問が放送されます。質問に対する答えを，問題用紙に印刷されている４つの選択肢から選びます。

質問を予想しよう

放送を聞く前に，問題用紙に印刷されている選択肢を見て，質問を予想しましょう。

1	In England.	**2**	In the United States.
3	In Australia.	**4**	In Japan.

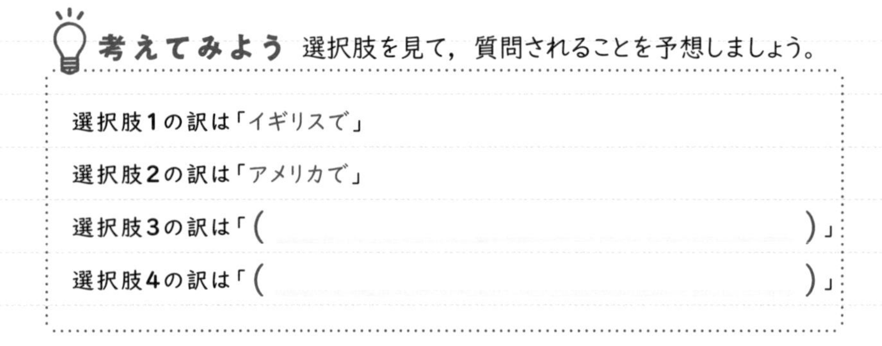

考えてみよう 選択肢を見て，質問されることを予想しましょう。

選択肢**1**の訳は「イギリスで」

選択肢**2**の訳は「アメリカで」

選択肢**3**の訳は「(　　　　　　　　)」

選択肢**4**の訳は「(　　　　　　　　)」

注意!

選択肢はすべて「国名」なので，「場所」について質問されるとわかります

音声を聞いて，問題を解いてみよう

TR 05

解答 (　　　　　)

読まれた英文 もう一度音声を聞き，空欄をうめましょう。

A: Where are you from, Ellen?

B: I was (　　　　) in England, but I grew up in Australia.

A: When did you come to Japan?

B: Three years ago. I lived in the United States before that.

QUESTION: (　　　　) was Ellen born?

注意!

bornを聞き取ることが重要です

日本語訳

A: 出身はどこなの，エレン?

B: イギリス生まれだけど，オーストラリアで育ったの。

A: 日本にはいつ来たの?

B: ３年前。その前はアメリカに住んでいたよ。

質問：エレンはどこで生まれましたか。

練習問題

TR 06

答えは別冊P26

対話と質問を聞き，その答えとして最も適切なものを**1**,**2**,**3**,**4**の中から一つ選びなさい。

(1)
1 20 dollars.
2 By tomorrow.
3 Next Saturday.
4 For a school trip.

1 2 3 4

(2)
1 The stadium.
2 City Museum.
3 The station.
4 The blue line.

1 2 3 4

(3)
1 Last summer.
2 Asakusa.
3 Twice.
4 For the first time.

1 2 3 4

(4)
1 One hour.
2 Two hours.
3 Three hours.
4 Four hours.

1 2 3 4

(5)
1 To tell him to take a camera.
2 To tell him to get some books.
3 To tell him to take a message.
4 To tell him to do field work.

1 2 3 4

(6)
1 10 dollars.
2 15 dollars.
3 20 dollars.
4 30 dollars.

1 2 3 4

PART 34

リスニング第2部

会話の内容を聞き取る②

学習日 

★理解度
□カンペキ!
□もう一度
□まだまだ…

第２部では,２人の会話と，その内容についての質問が放送されます。
答えは，問題用紙に印刷されている４つの選択肢から選びます。

質問を予想しよう 放送を聞く前に，問題用紙に印刷されている選択肢を見て，質問を予想しましょう。

1	She is sick.
2	She is busy.
3	She has to study.
4	She has to help her mother.

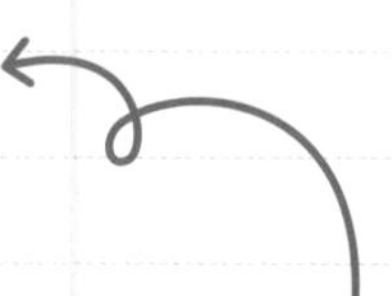

考えてみよう 選択肢を見て，質問されることを予想しましょう。

選択肢**1**の訳は「彼女は病気である」

選択肢**2**の訳は「彼女は忙しい」

選択肢**3**の訳は「彼女は（　　　　　）しなければならない」

選択肢**4**の訳は「彼女は（　　　　　）を助けなければならない」

注意!

選択肢はすべてSheのことなので,「彼女」の発言に注意して聞きます

音声を聞いて，問題を解いてみよう **解答**（　　　　　）

TR 07

読まれた英文 もう一度音声を聞き，空欄をうめましょう。

A: Hi, Beth. Let's go swimming after school.

B: Sorry, Mike. I can't.

A: Why not?

B: I have a（　　　　　）, so I want to go home early today.

QUESTION:（　　　　　）won't Beth go swimming with Mike today?

日本語訳

A:やあ，ベス。放課後泳ぎに行こうよ。

B:ごめんね，マイク。行けないの。

A:どうして?

B:風邪をひいたから，今日は早く家に帰りたいの。

質問:ベスはなぜ今日マイクと泳ぎに行かないのですか。

練習問題 TR 08

答えは別冊P27

対話と質問を聞き，その答えとして最も適切なものを**1**,**2**,**3**,**4**の中から一つ選びなさい。

(1)
1 Kyoto.
2 Osaka.
3 Tokyo.
4 Sapporo.
① ② ③ ④

(2)
1 A steak and rice.
2 A steak and coffee.
3 A steak, bread and coffee.
4 A steak, rice and coffee.
① ② ③ ④

(3)
1 After class today.
2 Tonight.
3 Tomorrow.
4 Next week.
① ② ③ ④

(4)
1 Go to the theater.
2 Go to the beach.
3 Go to Christy's house.
4 Go to John's house.
① ② ③ ④

(5)
1 By car.
2 By train.
3 By bus.
4 On foot.
① ② ③ ④

(6)
1 David's.
2 Ashley's.
3 Nicole's.
4 Bob's.
① ② ③ ④

PART 35 リスニング第3部
英文の内容を聞き取る①

学習日

★理解度
□カンペキ!
□もう一度
□まだまだ…

リスニング第3部は，短い英文が放送されます。その後，英文の内容に関する質問が放送されるので，その答えを問題用紙に印刷されている選択肢の中から選びます。

質問を予想しよう 放送を聞く前に，問題用紙に印刷されている選択肢を見て，質問を予想しましょう。

1	Tennis.	**2**	Soccer.
3	Swimming.	**4**	Golf.

考えてみよう 選択肢を見て，質問されることを予想しましょう。

選択肢**1**の訳は「テニス」　選択肢**2**の訳は「サッカー」

選択肢**3**の訳は「(　　　　)」　選択肢**4**の訳は「(　　　　)」

注意!

選択肢はすべて「スポーツ」だとわかります

TR 09

音声を聞いて，問題を解いてみよう **解答** (　　　　)

読まれた英文 もう一度音声を聞き，空欄をうめましょう。

Steve likes sports. He plays tennis and golf with his family. He has a swimming lesson on weekends. But his (　　　　) sport is soccer. He always enjoys watching it on TV.

QUESTION: (　　　　) sport does Steve like best?

日本語訳

スティーブはスポーツが好きです。彼は家族と一緒にテニスとゴルフをします。週末に水泳を習っています。でも，彼のお気に入りのスポーツはサッカーです。いつもテレビで見て楽しんでいます。

質問：スティーブはどのスポーツがいちばん好きですか。

答えは別冊P29

英文と質問を聞き，その答えとして最も適切なものを**1**,**2**,**3**,**4**の中から一つ選びなさい。

(1)
1 Take a photo.
2 Play the violin.
3 Turn off the cellphones.
4 Buy food and drinks.

① ② ③ ④

(2)
1 Climb the mountain.
2 Go hiking.
3 Have a home party.
4 See some movies.

① ② ③ ④

(3)
1 One week.
2 Three weeks.
3 One year.
4 Three years.

① ② ③ ④

(4)
1 Gave the watch.
2 Lost the watch.
3 Looked at the watch.
4 Found the watch.

① ② ③ ④

(5)
1 Practice chorus.
2 Meet at the school.
3 Make lunch.
4 Watch the contest.

① ② ③ ④

(6)
1 Getting three camera lenses.
2 Buying a new smartphone.
3 Going on a short trip.
4 Taking photos.

① ② ③ ④

PART 36

リスニング第3部

英文の内容を聞き取る②

学習日

★理解度
□カンペキ！
□もう一度
□まだまだ…

リスニング第３部は，短い英文が放送されます。その後，英文の内容に関する質問が放送されるので，その答えを問題用紙に印刷されている選択肢の中から選びます。

質問を予想しよう

放送を聞く前に，問題用紙に印刷されている選択肢を見て，質問を予想しましょう。

1	Buy some salad.	**2**	Make breakfast.
3	Teach French to her.	**4**	Help her in the office.

注意！

選択肢はすべて「行動，動作」なので，「だれが何をするか」に注意して聞きます

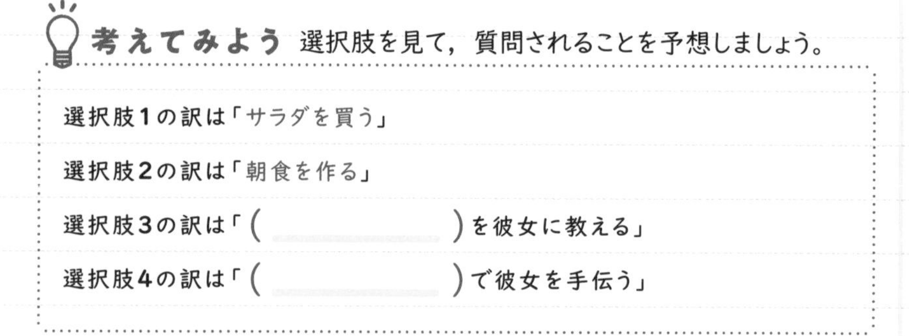

考えてみよう 選択肢を見て，質問されることを予想しましょう。

選択肢**1**の訳は「サラダを買う」

選択肢**2**の訳は「朝食を作る」

選択肢**3**の訳は「(　　　　　　)を彼女に教える」

選択肢**4**の訳は「(　　　　　　)で彼女を手伝う」

音声を聞いて，問題を解いてみよう

TR 11

解答 (　　　　　)

読まれた英文　もう一度音声を聞き，空欄をうめましょう。

I have to go to work earlier tomorrow. I won't have time to (　　　　　) breakfast, so I asked my daughter to do it. She's going to prepare French toast and salad. She's really helpful.

QUESTION: (　　　　　) did the woman (　　　　　) her daughter to do?

日本語訳

私は明日早く仕事に行かなければなりません。朝食を作る時間がないので，娘に頼みました。彼女はフレンチトーストとサラダを準備するつもりです。彼女は本当に助けになります。

質問：女性は娘に何をするように頼みましたか。

練習問題 TR 12

答えは別冊P30

英文と質問を聞き，その答えとして最も適切なものを**1**,**2**,**3**,**4**の中から一つ選びなさい。

(1) **1** Spring.
2 Summer.
3 Fall.
4 Winter.

1 2 3 4

(2) **1** At 1:00.
2 At 1:15.
3 At 1:30.
4 At 1:45.

1 2 3 4

(3) **1** How to go to school.
2 Sports such as soccer and baseball.
3 His friend living next to him.
4 Going to Australia next month.

1 2 3 4

(4) **1** Tuesday.
2 Wednesday.
3 Thursday.
4 Friday.

1 2 3 4

(5) **1** Ten minutes.
2 Thirty minutes.
3 Forty-five minutes.
4 One hour.

1 2 3 4

(6) **1** Selling necklaces.
2 Doing a part time job.
3 Taking care of her sister.
4 Helping his girlfriend.

1 2 3 4

模擬試験

答えは別冊 P 32～43

本番と同じ形式の模擬試験です。
本番の練習になるように，次の3つを守って解きましょう。
① 筆記試験（96～105ページ）は，65分で解く。
② リスニングテスト（106～109ページ）は，音声を止めないで解く。
③ 筆記試験からリスニングテストまで通して解く。
※解答用紙は別冊の最後のページにあります。

1

次の *(1)* から *(15)* までの（　　）に入れるのに最も適切なものを **1**, **2**, **3**, **4** の中から一つ選び，その番号のマーク欄をぬりつぶしなさい。

---

(1) These two bags look the same. What's the (　　　) between them?

1 tournament　**2** difference　**3** action　**4** promise

(2) We don't have to run, Steve. We have (　　　) time to catch the next bus.

1 quick　**2** hot　**3** enough　**4** clear

(3) ***A:*** Henry, can you pass me the (　　　) on the table? I need them to open this box.
B: OK. Here you are.

1 staplers　**2** stores　**3** scissors　**4** shoes

(4) ***A:*** Excuse me. I'm looking for toys for my daughter.
B: You can find them on the fourth (　　　), sir.

1 floor　**2** lesson　**3** introduction　**4** schedule

(5) ***A:*** What are you reading, Fred?
B: It's a new (　　　) by my favorite writer. I got it yesterday.

1 bicycle　**2** suitcase　**3** language　**4** novel

(6) ***A:*** Is Ted in the hospital? What (　　　)?
B: He was hit by a car this morning.

1 changed　**2** happened　**3** explained　**4** baked

(7) The Italian restaurant is over there. We have to (　　　) the street.

1 cross　**2** catch　**3** draw　**4** save

(8) ***A:*** Excuse me. Where is the post office?

B: It's near here. Go straight and (　　　) right at that corner.

1 order　**2** turn　**3** pay　**4** decide

(9) Last night, I studied until late. Now, I'm (　　　) for the test.

1 wrong　**2** delicious　**3** alone　**4** ready

(10) ***A:*** Is your sister (　　　) in baseball?

B: Yes. She often goes to the stadium.

1 worried　**2** interested　**3** hit　**4** held

(11) ***A:*** I baked a cherry pie today. Would you like to try it?

B: Thank you, Monica. A (　　　) of it sounds good.

1 list　**2** table　**3** slice　**4** club

(12) ***A:*** How long do I need to wait for the next train?

B: Oh, just a (　　　) of minutes.

1 couple　**2** bottle　**3** counter　**4** contact

(13) My cousin has a little black dog (　　　) Max.

1 call　**2** calls　**3** called　**4** calling

(14) It's not easy for Maria (　　　) Japanese.

1 speak　**2** speaks　**3** spoke　**4** to speak

(15) ***A:*** Do you know the woman (　　　) is talking with Jim?

B: She's his sister Kate.

1 who　**2** what　**3** whose　**4** where

次の *(16)* から *(20)* までの会話について，(　　　) に入れるのに最も適切なものを**1**, **2**, **3**, **4**の中から一つ選び，その番号のマーク欄をぬりつぶしなさい。

(16) ***Mother:*** Why is your sister crying?
Son: She was running on the way home, and (　　　)

1 it's sunny today.　　**2** that's her bag.
3 she'll be glad.　　**4** she fell down.

(17) ***Granddaughter:*** Can I have some cookies, Grandma?
Grandmother: Of course, Sally. (　　　)

1 Help yourself.　　**2** You're right.
3 Try your best.　　**4** I don't think so.

(18) ***Boy:*** I have to finish my history report by Wednesday. (　　　)
Girl: I've just turned it in. I spent most of the weekend on it.

1 Do you like history?
2 Have you finished yours yet?
3 Who is your history teacher?
4 Have you ever been to Philadelphia?

(19) ***Man:*** How often do you visit Sapporo?
Woman: I go there (　　　)

1 twice a year.　　**2** for five days.
3 to enjoy seafood.　　**4** and Asahikawa this time.

(20) ***Customer:*** Could I have another cup of coffee?
Waiter: (　　　) I'll be right back with it.

1 Certainly.　　**2** May I help you?
3 Not so good.　　**4** Here is the menu.

次の掲示の内容に関して，*(21)* と *(22)* の質問に対する答えとして最も適切なもの，または文を完成させるのに最も適切なものを**1**, **2**, **3**, **4**の中から一つ選び，その番号のマーク欄をぬりつぶしなさい。

Hamilton Art Museum News

● Special Exhibition

The special exhibition of paintings by Canadian artists from the 19th and 20th century has just started!

Admission:

Adults: $2.00

Students: $1.00

Seniors (60 & over): Free

Children (18 & under): Free

● Guided Tours

Join a free guided tour with one of our gallery guides! Mini-tours are 30 minutes, and start at 2:30 p.m. on weekdays and at 11:00 a.m. on weekends. Highlight tours are 1 hour, and start at 1:00 p.m on weekends. Tours begin at the north door on the second floor.

We are open every day from 10:00 a.m. to 6:00 p.m.

For more information, visit our website at:

http://www.hamiltonartmuseum.com

(21) You will pay $2 to see the special exhibition, if you are

1 70 years old.

2 50 years old.

3 a student.

4 a gallery guide.

(22) What time do highlight tours begin?

1 At 10:00 a.m.

2 At 11:00 a.m.

3 At 1:00 p.m.

4 At 2:30 p.m.

次のEメールの内容に関して，***(23)*** から ***(25)*** までの質問に対する答えとして最も適切なもの，または文を完成させるのに最も適切なものを**1**, **2**, **3**, **4**の中から一つ選び，その番号のマーク欄をぬりつぶしなさい。

From: Mami Fujimoto
To: Eliza Williams
Date: November 27
Subject: I'm going to visit Sydney!

Hi Eliza!
How are you and your husband doing? Five years have already passed since I left Sydney. I've always wanted to come back. And finally, I can visit you again! As you know, I work for a Japanese company which has some offices in Australia, and I'm going to visit two of them. I am going to arrive first in Melbourne on the 14th of December. I'll have a meeting the next day. On the 16th, I'll move to Sydney. I'll have another meeting on the 17th and have to fly back to Japan that night. Do you have time on the 16th? I'd like to visit you then.
Write back soon,
Mami

From: Eliza Williams
To: Mami Fujimoto
Date: November 28
Subject: Welcome back!

Hi Mami!
Thank you so much for your e-mail. Yes, we'll be free on the 16th. My husband George stopped working last year, so we have more time than before. Now, we have another student from Japan named Haru in our house. She is studying business at a university. That's exactly the same as you five years ago. She'll be here until January next year, so you can meet her, too. She says she wants to ask you about getting a job in Japan, so please tell her your experience. Are you going to fly from Melbourne? We will pick you up at the airport. Please tell us the time of your arrival.
See you,
Eliza

(23) Mami will come to Sydney

1 for sightseeing.

2 to study business.

3 on business.

4 to see her sister.

(24) When will Mami leave Sydney?

1 On December 15th.

2 On December 16th.

3 On December 17th.

4 On December 18th.

(25) What is Haru doing in Sydney?

1 She is working for a Japanese company.

2 She is teaching Japanese.

3 She is looking for a house to live in.

4 She is studying at a university.

次の英文の内容に関して，*(26)* から *(30)* までの質問に対する答えとして最も適切なもの，または文を完成させるのに最も適切なものを**1**, **2**, **3**, **4**の中から一つ選び，その番号のマーク欄をぬりつぶしなさい。

Dream Catchers

If you go to the United States or Canada, you may find a dream catcher somewhere. It is a ring with a net like a spider's web,* and there is a hole in the middle of the net. Many people put dream catchers on the walls of their rooms to enjoy looking at them, but where did they come from?

The origin of dream catchers is from Ojibwa culture. Ojibwa is a tribe* who live in the United States and Canada. In the mid-1800s, people from Europe wrote that dream catchers were used to protect children from bad dreams.

Ojibwa people believe that dream catchers catch bad dreams, as spiders' webs catch insects. In the morning, the sun light hits the dream catchers and burns away the bad dreams. However, good dreams are able to pass through the webs and get to sleeping children. In this way, children can have only good dreams during the night.

Today, dream catchers have become more colorful. They are decorated* with many different materials. These dream catchers are very beautiful, so they are popular as souvenirs from the United States and Canada. On the other hand, it is not difficult to make a simple dream catcher, so children often create their own at school and put them on the classroom wall.

*spider's web：クモの巣
*tribe：部族
*decorate：～を飾る

(26) How do many people use dream catchers?

1 They enjoy looking at them in their rooms.

2 They take them to the United States or Canada.

3 They close the hole in the middle of the net.

4 They catch spiders and keep them inside.

(27) Who first made dream catchers?

1 People who moved to Canada.

2 Canadians who moved to Europe.

3 Ojibwa people in North America.

4 American people having children.

(28) In the mid-1800s, people from Europe wrote that

1 Ojibwa people made money by selling dream catchers.

2 Ojibwa children were afraid of dream catchers.

3 they were told how to make dream catchers by Ojibwa people.

4 the purpose of a dream catcher was to protect children.

(29) How do dream catchers work?

1 They create good dreams.

2 They take away bad dreams.

3 They bring something lucky.

4 They give good ideas.

(30) What is this story about?

1 A special event made to give dreams to children.

2 One of the most famous souvenirs around the world.

3 One way to protect children from spiders and insects.

4 A traditional product which is still popular today.

ライティング　（Eメール）

- あなたは，外国人の友達（Jane）から以下のEメールを受け取りました。Eメールを読み，それに対する返信メールを，[　　]に英文で書きなさい。
- あなたが書く返信メールの中で，友達（Jane）からの2つの質問（下線部）に対応する内容を，あなた自身で自由に考えて答えなさい。
- あなたが書く返信メールの中で[　　]に書く英文の語数の目安は，15語～25語です。
- 解答は，解答用紙のEメール解答欄に書きなさい。なお，解答欄の外に書かれたものは採点されません。
- 解答が友達（Jane）のEメールに対応していないと判断された場合は，0点と採点されることがあります。友達（Jane）のEメールの内容をよく読んでから答えてください。
- [　　]の下のBest wishes, の後にあなたの名前を書く必要はありません。

Hi,

Your little sister is so cute! I saw her at the supermarket with your mother today. How old is she? Do you have any other brothers or sisters? I wish I had a little sister, too.

Your friend,
Jane

Hi, Jane!

Thank you for your e-mail.

[解答欄に記入しなさい。]

Best wishes,

ライティング （英作文）

- あなたは，外国人の友達から以下の**QUESTION**をされました。
- **QUESTION**について，あなたの考えとその理由を２つ英文で書きなさい。
- 語数の目安は，25語～35語です。
- 解答は，解答用紙の英作文解答欄に書きなさい。なお，解答欄の外に書かれたものは採点されません。
- 解答が**QUESTION**に対応していないと判断された場合は，0点と採点されることがあります。**QUESTION**をよく読んでから答えてください。

QUESTION

Which do you like better, spring or summer?

Listening Test

3級リスニングテストについて

❶ このテストには，**第1部**から**第3部**まであります。

英文は第1部では一度だけ，第2部と第3部では二度，放送されます。

第**1**部	イラストを参考にしながら対話と応答を聞き，最も適切な応答を**1**, **2**, **3**の中から一つ選びなさい。
第**2**部	対話と質問を聞き，その答えとして最も適切なものを**1**, **2**, **3**, **4**の中から一つ選びなさい。
第**3**部	英文と質問を聞き，その答えとして最も適切なものを**1**, **2**, **3**, **4**の中から一つ選びなさい。

❷ ***No. 30***のあと，10秒すると試験終了の合図がありますので，筆記用具を置いてください。

第1部

No. 1

TR 14

No. 2

TR 15

No. 3

TR 16

No. 4

TR 17

No. 5

TR 18

No. 6

TR 19

No. 7

TR 20

No. 8

TR 21

No. 9

TR 22

No. 10

TR 23

第2部

No. 11

TR 25

1 Korean.
2 Chinese.
3 Japanese.
4 Italian.

No. 12

TR 26

1 At 8:55.
2 At 9:00.
3 At 9:55.
4 At 10:00.

No. 13

TR 27

1 10 minutes.
2 40 minutes.
3 60 minutes.
4 70 minutes.

No. 14

TR 28

1 He can't find his table.
2 He didn't drink coffee.
3 He lost his watch.
4 He couldn't sleep last night.

No. 15

TR 29

1 Go to a restaurant.
2 Cook dinner.
3 Order a pizza.
4 Wait for the mother.

No. 16

TR 30

1 A dentist.
2 A nurse.
3 A teacher.
4 A tour guide.

No. 17

TR 31

1 Study with Charles.
2 Invite her friends home.
3 Help her grandmother.
4 Go out with her family.

No. 18

TR 32

1 Mary.
2 Jeff.
3 Jeff's daughter.
4 Jeff's son.

No. 19

TR 33

1 France.
2 Spain.
3 Germany.
4 Italy.

No. 20

TR 34

1 $15.
2 $20.
3 $25.
4 $30.

第3部

No. 21

TR 36

1 Her father.
2 Her mother.
3 Her brother.
4 Her friends.

No. 22

TR 37

1 Last Friday.
2 Last Saturday.
3 This morning.
4 This afternoon.

No. 23

TR 38

1 Once.
2 Twice.
3 Three times.
4 Four times.

No. 24

TR 39

1 Five.
2 Six.
3 Eight.
4 Nine.

No. 25

TR 40

1 She'll walk her dog.
2 She'll clean her house.
3 She'll collect garbage.
4 She'll swim in the sea.

No. 26

TR 41

1 Hats.
2 Men's clothes.
3 Women's clothes.
4 Children's clothes.

No. 27

TR 42

1 17.
2 18.
3 19.
4 20.

No. 28

TR 43

1 His friend's dog.
2 His pet.
3 His school.
4 His paper bag.

No. 29

TR 44

1 Sunny.
2 Cloudy.
3 Rainy.
4 Snowy.

No. 30

TR 45

1 He's not good at math.
2 He'll be busy tomorrow.
3 He's sick in bed.
4 He has little time to study.

二次試験（面接）

出題形式の概要

① 面接委員から渡される「問題カード」を使用します。
② 問題カードの内容は以下の2つです。
- 30語程度の英文のパッセージ
- パッセージに関連したイラスト

③ 試験の流れは以下の通りです。
問題カードの黙読（20秒間）⇒ 問題カードの音読 ⇒ No. 1～No. 5の質問に解答する

二次試験（面接）の流れ

入室

- 係員の指示に従い，手荷物を持って面接室に入ります。
- 入室後，面接委員にあいさつしましょう（Hello. / Good morning.など）。

2 面接カードを渡す

- 面接委員の指示（Can I have your card, please?など）に従い，「面接カード」を手渡します。
- 面接委員の指示（Please sit down.など）に従い，着席します。
- バッグなどの手荷物は座席の脇に置きましょう。

3 氏名・受験級の確認と，英語でのあいさつ

- 面接委員が，あなたの氏名を英語で確認します（May I have your name, please?など）。
  ➡英語で答えましょう（My name is Saki Suzuki.など）。
- 面接委員が，あなたが受験する級を英語で確認します（Ms. Suzuki, this is the Grade 3 test, OK?など）。
  ➡英語で答えましょう（Yes.など）。
- 面接委員から，英語でのあいさつ（How are you today?など）があります。
  ➡英語で答えましょう（I'm fine.など）。

4 問題カードの受け取りと黙読

- 面接委員からパッセージ（英文）とイラストが印刷された「問題カード」が手渡されます。
  ➡Thank you.などと言って受け取りましょう。
- 面接委員の指示（First, please read the passage silently for 20 seconds.）に従い，20秒間，問題カードの英文を黙読します。
  ➡パッセージ（英文）の量は約30語です。

5 問題カードの音読

- 面接委員の指示（Now, please read it aloud.）に従い，問題カードのタイトルと英文を音読します。最初にタイトル（題名）を読むことを忘れないように注意しましょう。
- 発音だけでなく，文の意味を考え，文の区切りに注意して大きな声ではっきりと読みましょう。

6 質疑応答

- 面接委員から英語でNo. 1～No. 5の5つの質問が出されます。
- No. 1～No. 3の質問については，問題カードを見ながら答えてかまいません。
  No. 3の質問に答えたあと，面接委員から問題カードを裏返すように指示されます（Now, Ms. Suzuki, please turn over the card and put it down.など）。
  ➡問題カードを裏返して，No. 4とNo. 5の質問には問題カードを見ないで答えます。

7 問題カードの返却と退室

- No. 5の応答のあと，指示（OK, Ms. Suzuki, this is the end of the test. May I have your card back, please?など）に従い，問題カードを面接委員に返却します。
- 面接委員から試験終了の指示（You may go now.など）があります。

練習問題

答えは別冊 P 44

TR 46-51

問題カード 下の四角の枠内が受験者に渡される情報です。

Libraries

A lot of cities and towns in Japan have libraries. People can read or borrow many different kinds of books there, so libraries are popular places to visit. At some libraries, volunteers read some interesting stories to children.

Questions（質問）

No. 1　Please look at the passage. What can people do at libraries?

No. 2　Please look at the picture. How many boys are wearing glasses?

No. 3　Please look at the man. What is he looking at?

Now, Mr. / Ms. _____, please turn the card over.
→ 問題カードを裏返します。

No. 4　How do you usually go to school?

No. 5　Do you like to listen to music?
Yes. と答えた場合 → Please tell me more.
No. と答えた場合 → What do you like to do in your free time?

著者

松本恵美子　まつもと えみこ

順天堂大学講師、明治大学法学部兼任講師、中央大学総合政策学部兼任講師。上智大学大学院博士前期課程修了(言語テスティング/英語教授法)。資格試験対策では主にTOEFL、TOEIC、英検などを指導する。学生から社会人まで、目標突破へと導く指導が得意。また、全国の大学用教科書の執筆、監修を務める。著書多数。

書いて覚える
英検®3級　合格ノート 音声DL　改訂版

著　者　松本恵美子
発行者　清水美成
発行所　**株式会社 高橋書店**
〒170-6014 東京都豊島区東池袋3-1-1 サンシャイン60 14階
電話　03-5957-7103

ISBN978-4-471-27627-0　©MATSUMOTO Emiko　Printed in Japan

定価はカバーに表示してあります。

本書の内容についてのご質問は「書名、質問事項(ページ、内容)、お客様のご連絡先」を明記のうえ、郵送、FAX、ホームページお問い合わせフォームから小社へお送りください。
回答にはお時間をいただく場合がございます。また、電話によるお問い合わせ、本書の内容を超えたご質問にはお答えできませんので、ご了承ください。本書に関する正誤等の情報は、小社ホームページもご参照ください。

【内容についての問い合わせ先】
書　面　〒170-6014 東京都豊島区東池袋3-1-1 サンシャイン60 14階　高橋書店編集部
F A X　03-5957-7079
メール　小社ホームページお問い合わせフォームから　(https://www.takahashishoten.co.jp/)

【不良品についての問い合わせ先】
ページの順序間違い・抜けなど物理的欠陥がございましたら、電話03-5957-7076へお問い合わせください。
ただし、古書店等で購入・入手された商品の交換には一切応じられません。

PART 1

よく出る名詞①

学校・スポーツ

学習日

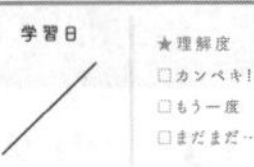

★理解度
□カンペキ!
□もう一度
□まだまだ…

英検３級では，学校に関する話題が多く出題されます。単語を「学校」「スポーツ」などのグループに分けて覚えましょう。

学校

スポーツ

(beginner) 初心者　(prize) 賞　(uniform) ユニフォーム，制服

My単語メモ
□
□
□
□
□

athlete	スポーツ選手	captain	主将，船長	coach	コーチ，指導者
contest	コンテスト	field	競技場，畑	goal	ゴール，目標
injury	負傷	locker	ロッカー	practice	練習
stadium	スタジアム	tournament	試合，トーナメント	winner	勝利者，優勝者

PART 2

よく出る名詞②

エンターテインメント・食べ物

学習日

★理解度
□カンペキ!
□もう一度
□まだまだ…

エンターテインメント

beach (ビーチ)　panda (パンダ)　zoo (動物園)

My単語メモ
□
□
□
□
□
□

band	(音楽の) バンド	concert	コンサート	event	イベント
festival	祭り	fun	楽しいこと	movie	映画
museum	美術館，博物館	nature	自然	theater	劇場，映画館

animal	動物	chimpanzee	チンパンジー	elephant	象
kitten	子猫	puppy	子犬	tiger	トラ

食べ物

練習問題

(1) 2　(2) 1　(3) 4　(4) 3　(5) 1　(6) 3

解説

(1) ジムはサッカーの試合を見ることが本当に好きなので，よくスタジアムに行きます。

(2) 私の姉は今年高校を終え，大学に行く予定です。

(3) A：あなたの辞書を使ってもいい？　今，いくつかの単語を調べる必要があるの。
B：いいよ。はい，どうぞ。

(4) A：君のチームは昨日のサッカーのトーナメントで勝ったそうだね。
B：うん。新しいコーチが僕らにいいアドバイスをくれたんだ。

(5) 女の子：来週，私たちのクラスにオーストラリアから生徒が来るのよ。
男の子：どうやって知ったの？
女の子：テイラー先生が昨日，私たちに彼女のことを話したの。
▶ **2** その生徒はどこの出身？　**3** その生徒に会った？
4 あなたはいつそれをしたの？

(6) 男の子：昨日，君は一日中テニスを練習したね。
女の子：明日，重要な試合があるの。とても緊張しているわ。
男の子：心配しないで。君はきっとうまくやるよ。
▶ **1** 君もね。　**2** 試合はどうだった？　**4** そのとおり。

練習問題

(1) 2　(2) 3　(3) 3　(4) 2　(5) 3　(6) 2

解説

(1) ジョンは来週ピアノのコンサートがあるので，演奏のためにとても一生懸命練習しています。

(2) 姉と私は犬が大好きです。彼らと遊ぶことは私たちを幸せにします。
▶ make ～ …「～を…にする」。「～」が代名詞のときは，「～を〔に〕」の形なのでusを選ぶ。

(3) A：映画はどうだった，エレン？
B：そうね，俳優たちはすばらしかったけど，話がつまらなかったわ。

(4) A：何か健康によいことをしていますか。
B：ええ。朝食前に犬と散歩することが私の習慣です。

(5) 先生：冬休みに何か予定はある，トム？
男の子：はい。ハワイに行く予定です。
先生：わあ，いいですね。
▶ **1** あなたは～を訪れることができます。　**2** 私は～の出身です。　**4** きっとあなたは～が気に入ります。

(6) 男の子：午後，うちの近くのパン屋さんに行こうよ。
女の子：いいわ。何時に待ち合わせる？
男の子：3時にうちに来て。
▶ **1** 午前中は忙しい。　**3** 君は何が買いたいの？
4 僕はそれがどこにあるか知らない。

PART 3

よく出る動詞①

活動する・コミュニケーションをとる

学習日 ／

★理解度
□カンペキ!
□もう一度
□まだまだ…

「活動する」動詞

3級では使われる動詞の種類が多くなります。自分で実際に活動している様子を思い浮かべてみましょう。

（ carry ） ～を運ぶ　（ clean ） ～をきれいにする　（ see ） ～を見る，～に会う

arrive	到着する	decide	(～を)決める	grow	育つ，～を育てる
jump	跳ぶ	learn	～を学ぶ	make	～を作る
move	移り住む，動く	push	～を押す	put	～を置く
relax	くつろぐ	throw	～を投げる	work	(機械が)作動する，働く

My単語メモ
□
□
□

覚えよう
〈make＋人＋形容詞〉で「人を～にさせる」

「コミュニケーションをとる」動詞

コミュニケーションでは積極的に相手にかかわることもあれば，自分が楽しんだり，相手を思いやったりする場合もあります。それぞれの単語について，自分が最近した行動を思い出してみましょう。

call ～に電話をする　（ enjoy ） ～を楽しむ　（ wait ） 待つ

覚えよう
take「（時間）がかかる」
cost「（お金）がかかる」

celebrate	～を祝う	contact	～に連絡をとる	give	(～に)…を与える
guess	推測する	invite	～を招待する	join	～に参加する
show	(～に)…を見せる	take	～を連れていく	tell	～に話す，～を教える

練習問題

(1) 3　(2) 1　(3) 2　(4) 4　(5) 1　(6) 3

解説

(1) 私はこの歌が好きです。いつも私を幸せな気分にします。

(2) 私はカメラを家に置いてきたので，今すぐ写真を撮ることができません。

(3) A：見て。お店のドアに掲示があるわ。
B：ええと，「本日閉店」と書いてあります。
▶ sayは「～と言う」のほかに「～と書いてある」という意味もあります。

(4) A：スピーチを始めるときは，何と言ったらいい?
B：例えば，「みなさん，こんにちは。自己紹介をさせてください。」
▶ **1** ～を見る　**2** 決心する　**3** ～を招待する

(5) 女の子：あの本はもう読んだ?
男の子：まだだけど，今日図書館に返さなきゃならない。
女の子：たぶん，もう一度借りることができるわ。
▶ **2** おもしろかったから，本当に気に入ったよ。 **3** 母が私にそれを買ってくれた。 **4** 彼はそれを50年前に書いた。

(6) 男性：この小包を北海道に送りたいのです。いつ着きますか
女性：3日かかります。
▶ **1**　2000円かかります。 **2**　電車は午後5時に出発します。 **4** タクシーに乗るべきです。

PART 4

よく出る動詞②

気持ちを表す

学習日 ／

★理解度
□カンペキ!
□もう一度
□まだまだ…

気持ちを表す動詞

（ find ） ～を見つける，～とわかる　（ hope ） 望む　（ smell ） においがする

believe	(～を)信じる	expect	～を予期する
feel	～を感じる	need	～を必要とする
taste	～の味がする	understand	～を理解する

My単語メモ
□
□
□
□
□
□

反対の意味とセットで覚える動詞

次の動詞は，反対の意味の動詞とセットで覚えると記憶に残りやすく，思い出しやすくなります。

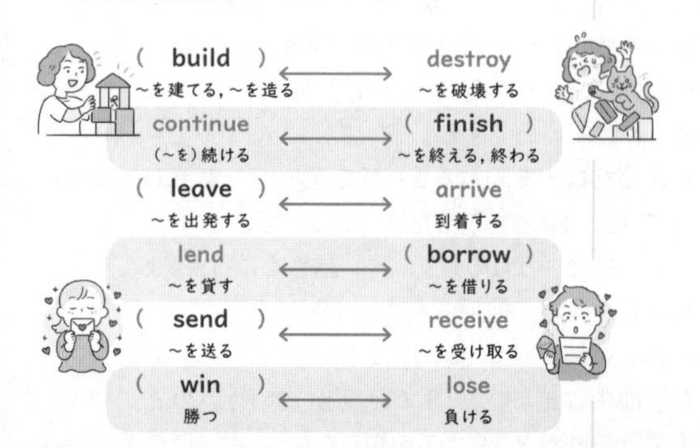

（ build ） ～を建てる，～を造る ⟷ destroy ～を破壊する
continue (～を)続ける ⟷ （ finish ） ～を終える，終わる
（ leave ） ～を出発する ⟷ arrive 到着する
lend ～を貸す ⟷ （ borrow ） ～を借りる
（ send ） ～を送る ⟷ receive ～を受け取る
（ win ） 勝つ ⟷ lose 負ける

練習問題

(1) 1　(2) 2　(3) 4　(4) 2　(5) 3　(6) 1

解説

(1) ジュディは英語を速く話したので，私は彼女の言葉を理解することができませんでした。
▶ **2** 走る　**3** ～を意味する　**4** ～を投げる

(2) A：明日，高校最後の試合があります。
B：君は3年間熱心に練習してきた。私は君が勝てると信じている。

(3) A：今朝はどんな気分ですか，ナンシー?
B：ずっとよくなっているわ，ママ。今日は学校へ行けると思うわ。

(4) A：マークの誕生日がもうすぐね。彼にプレゼントを買うのを忘れないで。
B：ありがとう，覚えておくよ。

(5) 女性：どうしたの?　調子が良くなさそうよ，フレッド。
男性：今日は1日中とても忙しかったから，少し疲れているんだ。
女性：どうぞ休んで。
▶ **1** 何をしているの?　**2** よさそうね。　**4** がんばって。

(6) 女の子：ボブ，私の新しいドレスをどう思う?
男の子：その色はとても君に似合っているよ。
女の子：ありがとう。
▶ **2** どこへ行ったの?　**3** その名前は知らないな。
4 ウェブサイトをチェックするよ。

PART 5

よく出る熟語①

get, takeを使った熟語

学習日 ／

★理解度 □カンペキ! □もう一度 □まだまだ…

いくつかの語がセットになっているのが熟語です。基本の動詞getとtakeを使った熟語を覚えましょう。

My単語メモ
□
□
□
□
□
□

getを使った熟語

getの基本の意味は「得る」です。

get (cold) 寒くなる　get (hungry) 空腹になる　get on (～) 乗り物などに(乗る)

get away from ～	～から逃げる, ～を離れる	get dark	暗くなる
get home	帰宅する	get off (～)	(乗り物などを) 降りる
get to ～	～に着く	get well	(体調が) よくなる
get along with ～	～とうまくやる	get ～ a ride	～を車で送る

takeを使った熟語

takeの基本の意味は「取る」です。

take a (break) 休憩する　take a (picture) 写真を撮る　take care of your dog あなたの犬の(世話)をする

take a walk	散歩する
take dance lessons	ダンスのレッスンを受ける
take me to the amusement park	私を遊園地に 連れて いく
take part in the hiking	ハイキングに 参加 する
Our plane will take off soon.	私たちの飛行機は間もなく離陸します。
It took me 2 hours to get home.	私は帰宅するのに2時間かかりました。

PART 6

よく出る熟語②

goを使った熟語, 量を表す熟語

学習日 ／

★理解度 □カンペキ! □もう一度 □まだまだ…

いくつかの語がセットになっているのが熟語です。基本の動詞goを使った熟語と,「量を表す熟語」を覚えましょう。

My単語メモ
□
□
□
□
□
□

goを使った熟語

goの基本の意味は「行く」です。

go on a trip (旅行)に出かける　go to (bed) 寝る

go for a walk	散歩 に行く
go shopping	買い物に行く
go straight	まっすぐに行く
go to the doctor	医師に診てもらいに行く

注意!
see a doctor「医者に行く」とも言います

量を表す熟語

water(水)は形のない液体なので, 1つ, 2つとは数えません(sをつけて複数形にしません)。数えられない名詞を「不可算名詞」といいます。なんとbread(パン)も不可算名詞です。パンはどんな形でも存在できますし, いくら切ってもパンだからです。水はグラスに入った形, パンは切った形で数えます。

覚えよう
milk(牛乳)やcoffee(コーヒー)などの飲み物や, paper(紙)なども不可算名詞です

a few ～	2, 3の～
a glass of ～	グラス1杯の～
a lot of ～	多くの～
a number of ～	多くの～, 多数の～
a piece of ～	ひと切れの～

練習問題

***(1)* 2　*(2)* 4　*(3)* 3　*(4)* 1　*(5)* 3　*(6)* 1**

解説

(1) 部屋を出るときは明かりを消してください。
▶ turn off ～で「(水道, ガス, 明かりなど) を消す〔止める〕」という意味。

(2) スミス先生は午後, 会議に参加するつもりです。
▶ take part in ～で「～に参加する」という意味。

(3) A：あなたの夢は何ですか。
B：大きくなったら, プロのサッカー選手になりたい。
▶ grow upで「成長する, 大人になる」という意味。

(4) A：ケビンから連絡はあった?
B：ううん。今も彼からのEメールを待っているの。
▶ hear from ～「～から連絡がある」

(5) 女の子：新しい町での生活はどう?
男の子：いいよ。隣人たちは僕に親切だから, 彼らとうまくやっているよ。
▶ **1** 来年またそこを訪れるよ。 **2** まだ彼らに会ったことがない。 **4** そこに着くことができなかったよ。

(6) 男の子：君は教科書をさがしていたね。見つけたの?
女の子：ええ。別のかばんの中にあったわ。
▶ **2** どこにも見えなかった。 **3** いいかばんを買えたわ。 **4** それはおもしろいと思いません。

練習問題

***(1)* 2　*(2)* 4　*(3)* 3　*(4)* 1　*(5)* 2　*(6)* 3**

解説

(1) 最初は, その仕事は私たちには難しすぎると思いましたが, 今はうまくできています。
▶ at firstで「最初は」という意味。

(2) 私はいつも仕事へ行く途中でコーヒーを1杯買います。
▶ on one's way to ～「～へ行く途中で」

(3) A：ウィルソンさんを見ましたか。
B：ええ, たった今, 事務所から走って出て行きました。いつものように忙しそうでした。
▶ as usualで「いつものように」という意味。

(4) A：私は将来映画監督になりたい。
B：あなたの夢が実現するといいわね。
▶ come trueで「実現する」という意味。

(5) 男性：息子は5歳。彼はほとんどの国旗を覚えています。
女性：すごいわ。記憶力がいいのね。
▶ **1** 彼は風邪をひいているかも。 **3** 彼はあなたと楽しい時をすごしました。 **4** 彼はそこへ行ったことがない。

(6) 母親：ボブ, これらの箱を車に運びたいの。手を貸してくれる?
息子：いいよ, ママ。全部運ぶよ。
▶ **1** あなたを乗せてあげられない。 **2** 私たちはバスに乗らなければならない。 **4** 帽子を脱いでください。

PART 7

比較

比べる文

学習日

★理解度
□カンペキ！
□もう一度
□まだまだ…

PART7からは文法の問題に入ります。

考えてみよう 次の3人の中で，一番背が高いのはだれか英語で書きましょう。（ Nancy ）

①原級 Mike is as tall （ as ） Jim. マイクはジムと同じくらい背が高い。

-er, -estがつかない元の形

②比較級 Nancy is （ taller ） than Mike . ナンシーはマイクよりも背が高い。

比較級（-er）＋than＋比べる人

③最上級 Nancy is the （tallest） of the three .

最上級（-est）＋of や in

ナンシーは3人の中で最も背が高い。

よく出る形容詞の，比較級・最上級の形を覚えましょう。

基本の変化 比較級は -er，最上級は -est をつけます。

原級	比較級	最上級
long（長い）	longer	longest
tall（背が高い）	taller	tallest

長い語の変化 -er，-est をつけると長すぎて発音しにくいので，前に more，most をつけます。

原級	比較級	最上級
beautiful（美しい）	more beautiful	most beautiful
expensive（高価な）	more expensive	most expensive

不規則な変化 一つ一つ覚えておきましょう。

原級	比較級	最上級
good（良い），well（上手に）	better	best
bad（悪い），ill（病気の）	worse	worst
many（数が多い），much（量が多い）	more	most
little（少ない）	less	least

覚えよう
よく出題されるので，しっかり覚えよう

24

PART 8

過去形と現在完了形

動詞の形に注意する

学習日

★理解度
□カンペキ！
□もう一度
□まだまだ…

3級を受験するみなさんが難しいと感じる文法の一つに，「過去形」と「現在完了形」の違いがあります。

過去形 現在から切り離された過去を表します。

Cathy went to the shopping mall last week.

動詞の過去形

キャシーは先週ショッピングモールに行きました。

「過去のある時点」で，キャシーがショッピングモールに行ったことを表しています。「現在」についてはわかりません。

覚えよう
否定文は
〈have／has not ＋過去分詞〉

現在完了形〈have／has ＋過去分詞〉

「現在」に影響を与えている「過去」を表します。

①「～してしまった」 動作の完了，その結果としての現在の状態を表します。

My uncle （ has ）（ gone ） to England on business.

〈has ＋過去分詞〉

おじは仕事でイギリスに行ってしまいました。

②「ずっと～している」 現在までの継続を表します。

They have been （ married ） for ten years.

〈have ＋過去分詞〉 「10年間」

彼らは10年間ずっと結婚しています（＝結婚してから10年になります）。

現在完了形（継続）の文には，下のような期間を表す語がつきます。

for ten years	10年間	since 2010	2010年以来

注意！
have gone to
「～へ行ってしまった」
have been to
「～へ行ったことがある」

③「～したことがある」 現在までの経験を表します。

I （ have ）（ read ） this book many times.

〈have ＋過去分詞〉

この本を何度も読んだことがあります。

26

練習問題

(1) 2　***(2)*** 4　***(3)*** 1　***(4)*** 3　***(5)*** 1　***(6)*** 3

解説

(1) この冬は昨年の冬より暖かかったので，ほとんど雪は降りませんでした。

▶ thanがあるので，比較級warmerを入れます。

(2) お互いに助け合うことはすべての中で一番大切なことです。

▶ importantの最上級は，前にmostを置きます。

(3) A：私とテニスをしない？

B：したいけど，君ほど上手にできないな。

A：いいのよ。楽しい時間になるわよ。

▶ not as ～ as ...で「…ほど～でない」という意味。

(4) A：昨日見たミュージカルはどうだった？

B：今まで見た中で一番良かったよ。

▶ good「良い」の最上級はbestです。

(5) 男の子：ピザを作るのは難しそうだ。

女の子：あまり難しくないわ。私にはケーキを作るより簡単よ。

男の子：じゃあ作ってみたい。作り方を教えてよ。

▶ **2** 作るために多くの食べ物を買わなくちゃ。 **3** 家の近くのおいしいレストランを知ってるわ。 **4** 難しいので作るのをあきらめたの。

(6) 母親：買い物に行きましょう，メアリー。できるだけ早く用意しなさい。

メアリー：ええ，今行くわ，ママ。

▶ **1** 雪が降っているから出かけられない。 **2** またね。 **4** あなたは忙しすぎて一緒に行けないわ。

練習問題

(1) 3　***(2)*** 3　***(3)*** 4　***(4)*** 2　***(5)*** 2　***(6)*** 1

解説

(1) ジムはもう自分の部屋をそうじしました。

▶ 現在完了（完了）の文。過去分詞cleanedを入れます。

(2) ここに父が先月京都で撮った写真があります。

▶ last monthがあるので，過去形tookを入れます。

(3) A：今までにロンドンに行ったことはある？

B：ええ，2回。

▶ 現在完了（経験）の文。have been to ～は「～に行ったことがある」。be動詞の過去分詞beenを使います。

(4) A：あなたのお兄さんは大学生のようね。

B：本当？　実際は高校生だよ。

▶ 付加疑問の文。主語がyour brotherで一般動詞の肯定文なので，doesn'tを入れます。

(5) 女の子：昨夜私が電話したとき，あなたは何をしていたの？

男の子：お風呂に入っていたよ。だから，電話に出られなかったんだ。

▶ **1** 夕食後テレビを見なかった。 **3** すみません，遅れます。 **4** まだ夕食を食べていません。

(6) 男の子：日本での滞在を楽しんでいるよ。東京が大好きさ。

女の子：よかった。どのくらい東京にいるの？

男の子：1週間たったよ。

▶ **2** いつオーストラリアに帰るの？ **3** 今どこに滞在しているの？ **4** 滞在中に何をしたい？

PART 9

進行形

現在進行形と過去進行形

学習日

★理解度
□カンペキ!
□もう一度
□まだまだ…

現在進行形「～しています」 be動詞（am, is, are）のあとに，動詞のing形を続けると「現在進行形」を表します。現在進行形とは「今，進行している動作」のことで，「～しています」という意味になります。

現在進行形 I（ am ）watching TV now.
〈be動詞+動詞のing形〉
私は今テレビを見ています。

現在進行形 Mark（ is ）(playing) the piano.
マークはピアノを演奏しています。

否定文 I am（ not ）watching TV now.
私は今テレビを見ていません。

疑問文 （ Is ）Mark playing the piano?
マークはピアノを演奏していますか。

覚えよう
疑問文はbe動詞を前に出します

過去進行形「～していました」 be動詞の過去形（was, were）のあとに，動詞のing形を続けると「過去進行形」を表します。過去進行形とは「過去に進行中だった動作」のことで，「～していました」という意味になります。

過去進行形 My mother（ was ）cooking breakfast for me.
〈be動詞の過去形+動詞のing形〉
母は私のために朝食を作っていました。

否定文 My mother was（ not ）cooking breakfast for me.
母は私のために朝食を作っていませんでした。

疑問文 （ Was ）my mother cooking breakfast for me?
母は私のために朝食を作っていましたか。

練習問題

(1) 1 **(2)** 3 **(3)** 1 **(4)** 2 **(5)** 4 **(6)** 2

解説

(1) ラジオの音量を下げてね。赤ちゃんが今，眠っているの。
▶ nowがあるので，現在進行形の文にします。

(2) 公園を歩いていたとき，突然雨が降り始めました。
▶ walkingを入れて過去進行形の文にします。

(3) A：今，何を読んでいるの，ケン？　英語の教科書？
B：いや，英語で書かれた漫画本だよ。簡単なんだ。
▶ be動詞areを入れて現在進行形の文にします。

(4) A：マーク，どこへ行くの？　駅まで乗せていってあげるよ。
B：ありがとう，ブラウンさん。僕は午後9時の電車に乗らなければなりません。
▶ areとing形で現在進行形の文にします。

(5) 母親：キョウコとの電話，長すぎよ。何を話していたの？
ジェーン：ごめんなさい，ママ。彼女は英語の宿題について尋ねたの。
▶ **1** 伝言を残したの？ **2** どちらさまですか。
3 どこで彼女と会ったの？

(6) 男の子：この前の日曜日，3時に劇場の前で君を見たよ。
女の子：そう？　そのときは友達を待っていたの。その日は演劇と，レストランでの食事を楽しんだのよ。
▶ **1** 先週の日曜日は外出しなかった。 **3** 何時にそこへ行くつもり？ **4** それは不可能よ。

PART 10

未来

willとbe going to ～

学習日

★理解度
□カンペキ!
□もう一度
□まだまだ…

未来を表す表現には，willとbe going to ～があります。

willの意味：客観的なこれから起こる出来事「～でしょう」，
自分の意思「～するつもり」
be going to ～の意味：自分が「～する予定です，きっと～しそうです」

注意!
違いを理解しておこう

willを使った未来の表現「～でしょう」「～するつもり」

未来の文を作るときにはwillを置き，動詞は原形にします。動詞がbe動詞（am, is, are）の場合は，原形のbeになります。

現在形 He is rich. 彼はお金持ちです。
↓
未来 He will（ be ）rich someday. 彼はいつかお金持ちになるでしょう。
〈will+動詞の原形〉

未来 I（ will ）drive you to the station.
駅まで車で送るつもりです[送ってあげるよ]。

覚えよう
will notを短縮してwon'tになります

未来の文は，tomorrow（明日に），in the future（将来に）などの未来を表す語句と一緒に使うことが多いです。

否定文 He（ won't ）be rich. 彼はお金持ちにならないでしょう。

疑問文 （ Will ）he be rich someday? 彼はいつかお金持ちになるでしょうか。

be going to ～を使った未来の表現「～する予定です」

be going toのあとには，動詞の原形を続けます。

現在形 I stay home. 私は家にいます。
↓
未来 I（ am ）(going)（ to ）stay home tomorrow.
動詞の原形
私は明日，家にいる予定です。

否定文 I am（ not ）going to stay home tomorrow.
私は明日，家にいる予定ではありません。

疑問文 （ Are ）you going to stay home tomorrow?
あなたは明日，家にいる予定ですか。

練習問題

(1) 2 **(2)** 3 **(3)** 2 **(4)** 4 **(5)** 1 **(6)** 3

解説

(1) 明日雨が降ったらどこへ行くつもりですか。
▶ tomorrowがあるので未来の文。willを入れます。

(2) 姉は来年，海外留学するつもりです。
▶ be going to *do*の文なのでto studyを入れます。

(3) A：日曜日に魚釣りに行く？
B：いや，行かないよ。今週末はしなければならない仕事がたくさんあるんだ。
▶ will notの短縮形won'tを入れます。

(4) A：北海道旅行の完璧な計画を立てたよ。
B：スキーをするつもりなの？
A：もちろん。
▶ be going to *do*の疑問文なのでareを入れます。

(5) 男の子：この夏休みは何をするつもり？
女の子：まだ決めてないけど，何か新しいことをしたいわ。
▶ **2** 泳いで楽しんだ **3** 退屈だった
4 楽しい時を過ごした

(6) 先生：あなたの将来の夢は何かを話してください。
生徒：病気の人々を助けたいので，看護師になります。
▶ **1** それは私には難しかった **2** 病院がありません
4 私はよい先生を探しています

PART 11 不定詞・動名詞

「～すること」

学習日 ★理解度 □カンペキ! □もう一度 □まだまだ…

不定詞〈to＋動詞の原形〉 〈to＋動詞の原形〉には，「～すること」「～するための」「～するために」の意味があります。

① 「～すること」 名詞のはたらき

To (study) English is very exciting.
〈to+動詞の原形〉「～すること」
英語を勉強することはとてもわくわくします。

② 「～するための」 形容詞のはたらき（前の名詞・代名詞を修飾します）

Do you want anything (to) drink?
〈to+動詞の原形〉「～するための」
飲むための何か(=何か飲み物)はいかがですか。

③ 「～するために」 副詞のはたらき（前の動詞を修飾します）

He worked hard (to) give her a good education.
〈to+動詞の原形〉「～するために」
彼は彼女によい教育を与えるために頑張って働きました。

動名詞〈動詞のing形〉 〈動詞のing形〉で，「～すること」と訳します。

I finished cleaning my room. 私は部屋をそうじすることを終えました。
動詞のing形

動名詞があとに続く動詞

enjoy	~ing	～することを楽しむ
finish	~ing	～することを終える(=～し終える)
stop	~ing	～することをやめる

不定詞があとに続く動詞

want	to ~	～したい
hope	to ~	～することを願う
decided	to ~	～することを決意する
need	to ~	～することが必要だ

覚えよう
動名詞が続く動詞，不定詞が続く動詞はしっかり整理して覚えよう

32

練習問題

(1) 3　(2) 4　(3) 2　(4) 3　(5) 2　(6) 4

解説

(1) ケンの父は彼に母をもっと手伝うように言いました。
▶〈tell+(人)+to *do*〉「(人)に～するように言う」

(2) ルーシーは怒っていたので，さよならも言わずに部屋を去りました。
▶ 前置詞 without のあとは動名詞にします。

(3) A：環境に何かよいことをするのは私たちにとって必要です。
B：賛成です。それについてもっと話しましょう。
▶〈It is ...(for 人)+to *do*〉「(人にとって)～するのは…だ」

(4) A：私は日本を去りますが，日本語を勉強し続けます。
B：そう聞いてうれしい。電話で日本語を話しましょう。
▶ keep *do*ing で「～し続ける」という意味。

(5) 母親：リサ，今晩パーティーに参加するの？
女の子：ええ，でも何を着たらいいかわからないの。
母親：わかったわ。一緒に選びましょう。あの赤いのはどう？
▶ **1** どこへ行くべきかわからない。 **3** 何時に始まるか教えて。 **4** 友達のカレンは来ません。

(6) 男の子：昨日の夏祭りはどうだった？
女の子：すてきだった。輪になって踊って楽しんだわ。
男の子：わあ，それは盆踊りだよ。楽しそうだな。
▶ **1** 雨だったので，外出できなかった。 **2** 多くの人が神社に来るそうだ。 **3** ボランティアで公園をそうじした。

PART 12 関係代名詞

関係代名詞の種類とはたらき

学習日 ★理解度 □カンペキ! □もう一度 □まだまだ…

関係代名詞には「接続詞」のように，2つの文をつないで1つの文にするはたらきがあります。また，「(代)名詞」のように，あとの節の中で主語や目的語になります。

関係代名詞の種類

先行詞＼役割	主格	所有格	目的格
人	who	whose	whom (who)
物事	which	whose	which
人・物事	that	―	that

① 主格の関係代名詞のはたらき

I know the girl. ＋ She is from Italy.
私は女の子を知っています。 彼女はイタリア出身です。

I know the girl (who) is from Italy.
先行詞「人」 関係代名詞
私はイタリア出身の女の子を知っています。

覚えよう
who以下がthe girlを修飾しています

② 所有格の関係代名詞のはたらき

I know the girl. ＋ Her father is a dentist.
私は女の子を知っています。 彼女の父親は歯医者です。

I know the girl (whose) father is a dentist.
先行詞「人」 関係代名詞
私は父親が歯医者である女の子を知っています。

③ 目的格の関係代名詞のはたらき

This is the movie. ＋ I saw it last night.
これは映画です。 私は昨夜それを見ました。

This is the movie (which) I saw last night.
先行詞「物」 関係代名詞
これは私が昨夜見た映画です。

注意！
目的格の関係代名詞は省略できます

34

練習問題

(1) 1　(2) 2　(3) 3　(4) 1　(5) 4　(6) 1

解説

(1) 私にはロンドンに住む友達がいます。
▶ 空所の前が「人」なので who を入れます。

(2) 私にはお父さんがプロサッカー選手の同級生がいます。
▶ 空所のあとが father なので whose を入れます。

(3) A：和食を出す良いレストランはある？
B：新しいすし屋が開店したそうよ。試してみるべきね。
▶ 空所の前が「物」なので which を入れます。

(4) A：この映画は気に入った？
B：ええ。今まで見た中で一番おもしろい映画よ。
▶ 関係代名詞 that 以下が movie を説明する文にします。

(5) 男性：フランス語を話す人を知りませんか。
女性：知ってるわ。ジョンが得意よ。
▶ **1** 彼はどこの出身ですか。 **2** 一度そこへ行ったことがある。 **3** どうやって学んだの？

(6) 男の子：昨日僕はサッカースタジアムへ行ったよ。ルーシー君はどう？
女の子：私はケイトと買い物に行ったの。これが私が昨日買ったネックレスよ。
男の子：とても美しくて君に似合ってる。
▶ **2** 彼女と出かけるのを楽しみにしている。 **3** 試合はわくわくした？ **4** 今週末の天気はどうなるかしら。

PART 13

受け身

受動態の基本

学習日 ／

★理解度
□カンペキ!
□もう一度
□まだまだ…

受け身の文は「～される」「～された」という意味を表し，文の形は〈be動詞(am, is, are, was, were)＋過去分詞〉です。

注意!
be動詞は，主語や時制に合わせて使い分けよう

通常の文 「(人／物) が～する」というように，行為をする人／物が主語です。

Karen (**wrote**) the letter last week. 先週カレンがその手紙を書きました。

受け身の文(受動態) 「(人／物) によって～される」というように，行為をされる人／物が主語になります。

The letter (**was**) (**written**) by Karen last week.
〈be動詞＋過去分詞〉 過去を表す語句

先週その手紙はカレンによって書かれました。

動詞の活用

- 過去形・過去分詞が同じ形　buy (～を買う) － bought － bought
- 原形・過去形・過去分詞がすべて同じ形　cut (～を切る) － cut － cut
- 原形・過去形・過去分詞がすべて違う形

原形	過去形	過去分詞
be (～である)	was／were	been
break (～を壊す)	broke	broken
eat (～を食べる)	ate	eaten
do (～をする)	did	done
drive (～を運転する)	drove	driven
give (～を与える)	gave	given
go (行く)	went	gone
know (～を知っている)	knew	known
speak (話す)	spoke	spoken
take (～を取る)	took	taken

覚えよう
過去形と過去分詞が違う動詞はよく出題されます

PART 14

分詞

現在分詞，過去分詞のはたらき

学習日 ／

★理解度
□カンペキ!
□もう一度
□まだまだ…

3級に出題される〈-ing形〉と〈-ed形〉はどちらも動詞が変化した形です。これらはそれぞれ「現在分詞」「過去分詞」と呼ばれ，形容詞としてはたらきます。

「形容詞としてはたらく」とは，前からも後ろからも名詞を修飾するということです。

現在分詞(-ing形)「～する／～している」

前から修飾 1語で名詞を修飾するとき

That was an (interesting) movie.
現在分詞 名詞

あれはおもしろい映画でした。

後ろから修飾 〈現在分詞＋語句〉で名詞を修飾するとき

A car (carrying) five people stopped at the intersection.
名詞 〈現在分詞＋語句〉

5人を乗せた車が交差点で停車しました。

覚えよう
短い(1語)ときは前から，長い(2語以上)ときは後ろから名詞を修飾します

過去分詞(-ed形)「～される／～されている」

前から修飾 1語で名詞を修飾するとき

There is a (broken) clock.
過去分詞 名詞

壊された時計があります。

後ろから修飾 〈過去分詞＋語句〉で名詞を修飾するとき

There is a clock (broken) by Laura.
名詞 〈過去分詞＋語句〉

ローラによって壊された時計があります。

注意!
過去分詞は，PART13の表で確認しよう

練習問題

(1) 4　(2) 2　(3) 3　(4) 2　(5) 1　(6) 4

解説

(1) この国ではフランス語と英語が話されます。
▶ 受け身の文。speakの過去分詞はspoken。

(2) 理科は週2回イトウ先生によって教えられます。
▶ 受け身の文。teachの過去分詞はtaught。

(3) A：私の自転車が昨日盗まれたの。悲しいわ。
B：警察に行くべきだよ。
▶ 過去の受け身の文。steal「盗む」の過去分詞はstolen。

(4) A：昨晩雪が降ったのですね?
B：ええ，驚きました。起きたとき，地面は雪で覆われていました。
▶ be covered with ～で「～で覆われている」という意味。

(5) 女の子：この寺はいつ建てられたの?
男の子：約400年前だよ。
▶ **2** いつでもここを訪れることができる。
3 1日に約300人。 **4** そこへ電車で行きました。

(6) 女の子：ケン，助けてくれる?
男の子：いいよ。どうしたの，ジュディ?
女の子：この手紙は日本語で書かれていて，読めないの。
▶ **1** 本屋は近い　**2** おもしろい物語を書きたい
3 ピアノのレッスンを受けるつもり

練習問題

(1) 3　(2) 2　(3) 1　(4) 4　(5) 4　(6) 3

解説

(1) 私の父は日本で作られた車を買いたいと思っています。
▶ 過去分詞を入れ，「作られた車」とします。

(2) 向こうでカトウ先生と話している少年はだれですか。
▶ -ingを入れ，「話している少年」とします。

(3) A：あなたのお姉さんによって焼かれたクッキーはとてもおいしい。
B：ありがとう。彼女はいつもおいしいスイーツを作るよ。
▶ 過去分詞を入れ，「焼かれたクッキー」とします。

(4) A：すみません。一番近いコンビニエンスストアはどこにありますか。
B：ごめんなさい，わかりません。門の前に立っている男性に尋ねてください。
▶ -ingを入れ，「立っている男性」とします。

(5) 男の子：この本はおもしろかったよ。作者は君の国で有名なの?
女の子：ええ。私は彼によって書かれたすべての小説が好きよ。
▶ **1** どこで買ったのか教えて。 **2** 君はいつ読んだの?
3 タイトルが何か思い出せない。

(6) ブラウン先生：サリー，上手に歌う生徒を知ってる?
女の子：はい。キョウコはクラスで一番上手に歌います。
▶ **1** 私はピアノを弾くのが得意ではありません。 **2** 私は日本のポップ音楽を聞くのが好きです。 **4** 私は若い人々に愛されている多くの歌を知っています。

PART 15 会話表現①
勧誘する・何かをお願いする

学習日

★理解度 □カンペキ! □もう一度 □まだまだ…

would likeを使った表現

勧誘・依頼の中では，would likeがよく出題されます。I would like to ～は，I want to ～の丁寧な表現です。want to ～は自分のやりたいことをストレートに伝えるのに対して，would like to ～は相手の助けを求める「もしよかったら～」のニュアンスがあります。

依頼 I（would）like some tea, please.
紅茶をいただけますか。

勧誘 Would you（ like ）to join us tonight?
今夜，仲間に加わりませんか。

勧誘・依頼に対する答え方

勧誘・依頼に対する答え方には「受ける」「断る」「どちらとも言えない」など，さまざまな正解があります。

覚えよう
答え方までセットで覚えましょう

Why don't we have dinner together?
夕食をご一緒しませんか。

Of course.
いいですよ。

No problem.
いいですよ。

I'd be glad to.
喜んで。

Sure, I'd love to.
もちろん，喜んで。

How about calling John?
ジョンに電話してみてはどう?

Maybe next time.
次回はそうします。

My boss will help me. Thanks anyway.
上司が手助けしてくれます。ありがとうございます。

（Would）you like to see the house?
家をご覧になりますか。

I'm not sure.
どうでしょう。

I'll have to ask my wife.
妻に聞いてみないと。

40

PART 16 会話表現②
電話での会話

学習日

★理解度 □カンペキ! □もう一度 □まだまだ…

3級では会話問題やリスニング問題などで，電話での応答が出題されます。相手を呼び出してもらうときの表現や，相手が不在だったときの表現などを覚えておきましょう。

相手を呼び出すときの表現

電話をかける	電話を受ける
Hello, this is Wendell calling. こちらはウェンデルです。 ↓	
May I（ speak ）to Ms. White, please? ホワイトさんとお話しできますか。	→ Sure, hold on, please. もちろんです，お待ちください。
Is Dr. Powell there? パウエル医師はいますか。	→ Speaking. 私ですが。

相手が不在だったときの表現

電話をかける	電話を受ける
Can I talk with Melissa, please? メリッサと話せますか。	→ Sorry, she's on another line now. すみません，彼女は他の電話にでています。 → May I take a message? ご伝言を預かりましょうか。
→ That's okay. I'll call back later. 結構です。またかけなおします。	

電話でよく出るその他の表現

Hi, Eric. What's up? もしもし，エリック。どうしたの?	Who's calling? どちら様ですか。
Just a minute, please. 少々お待ちください。	Sorry, you have the（ wrong ）number. すみませんが，番号をお間違えです。

42

練習問題

(1) 3　(2) 1　(3) 4　(4) 2　(5) 2

解説

(1) 男の子：君のお姉さんについて教えてくれる?
女の子：いいわ。姉のケイトは大学生よ。
▶ **1** あなたは何人姉妹がいる?　**2** 私は犬2匹と猫1匹を飼っている。　**4** おばは昨年数学の先生になった。

(2) 女性：窓を開けましょうか。この部屋は少し暑いです。
男性：はい，お願いします。尋ねてくれてありがとう。
▶ **2** 何か食べるものはありますか。　**3** 私は熱があると思いますか。　**4** ラジオの音量を上げてくれませんか。

(3) 男の子：今日の午後，ボブへの誕生日プレゼントを買うつもりだ。
女の子：私もよ。一緒に買い物に行かない?
男の子：いい考えだね。
▶ **1** いい店を知らないの。　**2** 彼に何を買ったの?
3 ボブが何歳か教えて。

(4) 男の子：今日ラケットを持ってくるのを忘れたんだ。君のを借りてもいい?
女の子：ごめん，アレックス。1つだけ持っていて，今，使ってるの。
▶ **1** 君は1つ買うつもり?　**3** 何をしているの?　**4** どうしたの?

(5) 男の子：映画の券が2枚ある。今週末行かない?
女の子：行きたいけど土曜日は忙しいわ。日曜日はどう?
男の子：いいよ。日曜日は僕も都合がいい。
▶ **1** 映画館は好きじゃない。　**3** また今度。　**4** 土曜日にどこで会う?

練習問題

(1) 2　(2) 3　(3) 1　(4) 4

解説

(1) 男の子：もしもし。ボブです。ジェーンと話せますか。
女の子：私よ。どうしたの，ボブ?
男の子：やあ，ジェーン。今日の午後はひま?
▶ **1** 君の電話番号は何?　**3** お会いできてうれしい。
4 電話してくれてありがとう。

(2) 男性：もしもし。
女性：もしもし，テイラーさん。キャシーはご在宅ですか。
男性：すみません，彼女は外出中です。1時間で戻ってくると思います。
▶ **1** ええ，今，家にいます。　**2** そのままお待ちください。
4 伝言は預かりませんでした。

(3) 男性：もしもし，スティーブ・ブラウンです。ウィルソンさんをお願いできますか。
女性：彼は今，会議中です。折り返すよう言いましょうか。
男性：結構です。あとでまたかけます。
▶ **2** 伝言を預かりましょうか。　**3** あなたに電話です。
4 10時に会うのはどうですか。

(4) 女性：もしもし。グリーンスーパーマーケットですか。
男性：すみませんが，こちらはスーパーマーケットではありません。番号違いです。
女性：ごめんなさい。間違えました。
▶ **1** あなたの番号を教えてください。　**2** 何を買う必要がありますか。　**3** 私たちの店へようこそ。

PART 17

会話表現③

旅行先・買い物での会話

学習日 ／

★理解度
□カンペキ!
□もう一度
□まだまだ…

リスニングや会話問題などでは，お店での店員と客とのやりとりも出題されます。

洋服を選ぶときの表現

店員	客
(**Welcome**) to our shop. May I help you? ようこそお越しくださいました。何かお探しですか。	I'm (**looking**) for a skirt. スカートを探しています。
We have some over there. How about this one? あちらにいくつかございます。これはいかがですか。	May I try this on? 試着できますか。
Certainly, ma'am. (←男性のときはsir) I'll show you the way. もちろんです，お客様。ご案内します。	

会計するときの表現

店員	客
You look good on it. お似合いです。	How (**much**) is this skirt? このスカートはいくらですか。
This is on sale. It's three thousand yen. セール中です。3000円です。	That's fine. I'll take this. それでいいです。これを買います。
Thank you. How would you like to (**pay**)? ありがとうございます。 お支払いはどうなさいますか。	Do you accept credit card? クレジットカードは使えますか。

PART 18

会話表現④

レストラン・食事での会話

学習日 ／

★理解度
□カンペキ!
□もう一度
□まだまだ…

レストランでの店員と客との会話も多く出題されます。注文から料理の提供まで，どんな場面かを想像しながら学習しましょう。

注文するときの表現

店員	客
Are you ready to (**order**), sir? お客様，ご注文はお決まりですか。	Yes. Could I have a beef steak? はい。ステーキをいただけますか。
Sure. How would you like your steak? かしこまりました。ステーキの焼き加減はどうなさいますか。	Medium, please. ミディアムでお願いします。
Would you like a salad with that? ご一緒にサラダはいかがですか。	

食後の表現

店員	客
Here's your coffee. Do you take sugar or milk? コーヒーをお持ちしました。 お砂糖とミルクはご利用ですか。	Just a little (**sugar**), please. 砂糖を少し入れてください。
Would you like some more (**bread**)? パンをまだ召し上がりますか。	No, thank you. I'm full. 結構です。おなかがいっぱいです。

ファストフード店での表現

店員	客
For here or to go? こちらでお召し上がりですか。お持ち帰りですか。	To go. Can I get a hamburger and a coffee? 持ち帰りで。ハンバーガー1つとコーヒーを1ついただけますか。
Which size would you like, small, medium or large? S, M, Lのどちらのサイズにしますか。	Small one, please. Sをください。

練習問題

(1) 3　(2) 1　(3) 4　(4) 1　(5) 2

解説

(1) 店員：いらっしゃいませ。
客：見ているだけです。ありがとう。
店員：必要があればお知らせください。
▶ **1** バス停はどこですか。 **2** 何時かわかりません。 **4** あなたがそれを気に入ってくれてうれしいです。

(2) 客：このシャツは私には大きすぎます。ほかのサイズを試してもいいですか。
店員：かしこまりました。こちらがより小さいものです。
▶ **2** このサイズを買うのを決めるべきですか。 **3** これで別の色はありますか。 **4** 僕にぴったりだと思う。

(3) 客：このかばんが気に入ったわ。いくらですか。
店員：20ドルです。
客：いいわ。買います。
▶ **1** かばんはいくつあるの？ **2** どのくらいよく来るの？ **3** いつそれを買ったの？

(4) 男の子：迷子になったと思う，カレン。どうしよう。
女の子：落ち着いて，ロジャー。地図を調べましょう。
男の子：そのとおりだ。ほらここにあるよ。
▶ **2** どこにいるかわからない。 **3** 何をすべきか教えて。 **4** あなたはどこへ行きたいの？

(5) 男の子：ニューヨークには見るべき場所がたくさんある。まずどこへ行くべきかな。
女の子：自由の女神像はどう？ 前に見たことある？
男の子：一度もない。見たいよ。
▶ **1** あなたはそれを何と呼ぶの？ **3** 私はちょうど見たばかりよ。 **4** そこへの行き方を教えて。

練習問題

(1) 2　(2) 3　(3) 1　(4) 4　(5) 2

解説

(1) ウェイター：ご注文はお決まりですか。
女性：はい。卵サンドイッチとコーヒーをお願いします。
ウェイター：わかりました。すぐお持ちします。
▶ **1** 注文を変えてもいいですか。 **3** メニューを見せてもらえますか。 **4** 今日の特別メニューは何ですか。

(2) 女の子：紅茶をお願いします。
ウェイター：かしこまりました。ほかには？
女の子：いいえ。以上です。
▶ **1** いくつ欲しいですか。 **2** 何をお飲みになりますか。 **4** すみませんが，十分持っていません。

(3) 女の子：美しい場所ですね，スミスさん。
女性：わが家へようこそ，ルーシー。自由に飲み物を飲んでね。
女の子：ありがとうございます。
▶ **2** よい旅を。 **3** ご招待ありがとう。 **4** 何か飲むものがほしいです。

(4) 男の子：ママ，夕食はカレーが食べたい。大好物さ。
母親：いいわ。では，お肉がないわ。今，スーパーマーケットに行ってくれる？
男の子：ごめん，今宿題をしなくてはならないんだ。
▶ **1** 昼食は何が食べたい？ **2** 作るために何が必要？ **3** 作り方を教えてくれる？

(5) 母親：メアリー，もっとクッキーをいかが？
女の子：結構よ，ママ。おなかがいっぱい。
▶ **1** 待ちきれない。 **3** あなたもね。 **4** 大丈夫？

PART 19

会話表現⑤

道案内の会話

学習日 ／

★理解度
□カンペキ！
□もう一度
□まだまだ…

3級では，目的地までの交通手段や道順を尋ねる表現が多く出題されます。答え方とあわせて覚えましょう。

迷ってしまったとき

I think we are lost.
私たちは迷ってしまったようです。

Let's ask someone.
だれかに聞こう。

声をかけるとき

道を尋ねる＆教える表現

尋ねる	教える
Could you tell me (how) to get to the Ueno station? 上野駅にはどうやって行けばいいか教えていただけますか。	Take the Yamanote Line at the Shinagawa station. 品川駅で山手線に乗ってください。
(Where) is Shinagawa Station? 品川駅はどこですか。	Go down this street. You'll get there in five minutes. この道を進んでください。5分で着きます。

48

練習問題

(1) 2　(2) 1　(3) 4　(4) 1　(5) 1

解説

(1) 男の子：この近くに薬局はありますか。
女の子：ええ。まっすぐ行けば，左側に見えます。
▶ **1** 私はすぐそこに行きます。
3 あなたは戻るべきです。
4 私は郵便局へ行くつもりです。

(2) 男の子：すみません。駅への道を教えていただけますか。
女の子：いいですよ。2番目の信号を右に曲がってください。そうすればあなたの真正面に見えます。
▶ **2** 私はいつ電車が来るかわかりません。
3 あなたが今どこにいるか教えてください。
4 この建物の名前を知っていますか。

(3) 男の子：病院はそんなに遠くありません。徒歩で行けます。
女の子：どのくらいかかりますか。
男の子：約10分です。
▶ **1** どうやってそこへ行けますか。
2 どのバスに乗るべきですか。
3 タクシーに乗ったらどうですか。

(4) 男の子：この電車は池袋駅に行きますか。
女の子：いいえ。次の駅で電車を乗りかえてください。池袋に向かう山手線に乗ってください。
▶ **2** あなたは池袋に来なければなりません。
3 駅はいくつありますか。
4 あなたはこの電車を降りる必要はありません。

(5) 男の子：すみません。この近くに郵便局はありますか。
女の子：ごめんなさい，わかりません。私はこのあたりは詳しくありません。
▶ **2** このあたりに銀行はありません。
3 私は何を買ったらいいですか。
4 あなたはどこの出身ですか。

PART 20

長文A

掲示・案内①

学習日

★理解度
□カンペキ!
□もう一度
□まだまだ…

3級で出題される長文は「掲示・案内」「メール」「説明文」の3種類です。まずは「掲示・案内」という短いお知らせ文を読んでいきましょう。

先に設問を読もう いきなり長文を読み始めるのではなく，まずは設問を読み長文の内容をつかみましょう。

設問1 What is the event held for?
（ **イベント** ）は何のために（**開かれる**）のですか。

選択肢
1 Throwing away bad tomatoes.
悪くなったトマトを投げ捨てるため。
2 Volunteering for a fire department.
消防署のためにボランティアをするため。
3 Raising money for people in need.
困っている人々のために（ **お金** ）を集めるため。
4 Watching people in a fight.
戦っている人々を見るため。

解答（ 3 ）

注意！
あてはまる日本語訳を考えて入れよう

設問2 People who take part in the event will
イベントに（**参加する**）人は

選択肢
1 clean the streets after the fight.
戦いのあと，通りを掃除するでしょう。
2 send money to hungry people.
飢えた人々にお金を送るでしょう。
3 hit other people with tomatoes.
（ **トマト** ）を他の人にぶつけるでしょう。
4 collect tomatoes from farms.
農場からトマトを集めるでしょう。

解答（ 3 ）

注意！
右ページの長文を読んで，設問に対する答えを4つの選択肢から選ぼう

長文を読んでみよう 設問をふまえて，お知らせ文を読んでいきましょう。

日本語訳

飢餓撲滅のためのトマトファイト
あなたは心配事を投げ捨ててしまいたいと願っていますか。毎年恒例の第15回トマト投げに参加してください。悪くなって食べることができない6,000ポンドのトマトがあります。それらをお互いに投げ合いませんか。ストレスがどこかに行ってしまうように感じるに違いありません。

日時：9月7日　土曜日
時間：午後3時30分から午後4時30分
場所：消防署の東側

戦いのあと，消防署がホースであなたを洗い流してくれます。チケットは10ドルです。あなたが支払ったお金はすべて世界の飢えた人々に食糧を与えるプログラムに渡ります。

戦いに参加するほど勇敢じゃない？　心配しないで。見るのを楽しんで寄付するだけでいいのです。

イベントの詳細をお知りになりたければ，ウェブサイトを訪れてください。

www.tomato-fight.com

練 習 問 題

***(1)* 4　*(2)* 2**

解 説

日本語訳

ワールドカップ観戦ツアー
第9回FIFA女子ワールドカップが，2023年の7月10日から8月20日まで，オーストラリアとニュージーランドで開催される予定です。32チームがカップを獲得するためにプレーします。第8回大会優勝のアメリカ合衆国チームは，チャンピオンのタイトルを守るために参加するでしょう。
すばらしい席でわくわくする試合を見るだけではなく，美しい国々を観光して楽しむ機会もあります。

パック商品：
豪華：オーストラリアのみ
豪華：ニュージーランドのみ
豪華：両方の国
お徳用：オーストラリアのみ

すべてのパック商品は飛行機チケット，朝食付きのホテルのクーポン，陸上の移動と試合のチケットを含んでいます。豪華パックは選手やコーチと一緒の3回の夕食を含んでいます。

パック商品の詳細と値段については，FIFAトラベルUSAのクリスティーンに連絡してください。
1-887-863-9681

(1) 試合はどこで行われますか。
▶ **1** オーストラリアで。
2 ニュージーランドで。
3 アメリカ合衆国で。
4 ニュージーランドとオーストラリアで。
本文最初の2行に注目。will be held ～ in Australia and New Zealand. とあります。

(2) お徳用パックを選んだ人は
▶ **1** 飛行機で旅行し損ねるでしょう。
2 ゲストと食事をし損ねるでしょう。
3 試合に参加し損ねるでしょう。
4 ホテルでの朝食を食べ損ねるでしょう。
Luxury packages include ～. の文に注目します。お徳用パックにはこれがありません。

PART 21

長文A
掲示・案内②

学習日 ／　★理解度 □カンペキ! □もう一度 □まだまだ…

「掲示・案内」という短いお知らせ文を読んでいきましょう。

先に設問を読もう いきなり長文を読み始めるのではなく，まずは設問を読み長文の内容をつかみましょう。

設問1 When will the language exams be held?
語学の試験は（ **いつ** ）行われますか。

選択肢
1 On Tuesday, June 8.
6月8日火曜日。
2 On Wednesday, June 9.
6月9日水曜日。
3 On Thursday June 10.
6月10日（ **木曜日** ）。
4 On Friday, June 11.
6月11日金曜日。

解答（ 3 ）

設問2 The exams in the other subjects will take place
他の教科の試験が行われるのは

選択肢
1 after economics exams are completed.
経済の試験が終わったあと。
2 in the cafeteria.
（**カフェテリア**）で。
3 in the meeting room.
会議室で。
4 before Friday, June 4.
6月4日金曜日以前。

解答（ 2 ）

覚えよう
設問の続きを選ぶ問題もあります

長文を読んでみよう 設問をふまえて，お知らせ文を読んでいきましょう。

日本語訳

学年末試験の日程

先生方が今年度末の試験の日程を決定しました。それぞれの日付でそれぞれの教科範囲が実施されます。学生たちは1日に1教科，それぞれの教科範囲の試験を受ければよいです。

日付	教科
6月8日火曜日	理科
6月9日水曜日	数学
6月10日木曜日	英語，スペイン語，フランス語，ドイツ語
6月11日金曜日	歴史，政治，経済
他の教科の試験は6月7日月曜日に実施されます。	

全生徒対象のすべての試験はカフェテリアで実施されます。試験期間中はカフェテリアを使うことができません。したがって代わりに会議室が開放されます。

試験についての質問があれば，必ず6月4日金曜日より前に先生へ尋ねるようにしてください。

練習問題

***(1)* 2　*(2)* 3**

解説

日本語訳

ミレニアムアフリカ祭り

またあの季節になりました!　アフリカの音楽と文化が大好きな人に加わってください。今年は，祭りの20周年を祝うためのたくさんの特別プログラムがあります。お見逃しなく!

日付：8月20日，21日，22日
時間：午前10時から真夜中まで
場所：ミレニアム公園
イベント：・ライブ演奏（ステージ上でのアフリカ音楽とダンス）
・大人と子ども向けのアフリカの太鼓教室
・ゲストトーク（アフリカの国々の歴史と文化について）
・アフリカの市場（アフリカの食べ物，飲み物と特産物）
チケット：1日15ドル，8歳以下の子どもは5ドル

祭りについてのより詳しい情報をお知りになりたい方は，私たちのウェブサイトを訪ねてください
www.millenniumafricanfest.com

(1) 母親，父親，8歳以下の2人の子どもが祭りに参加するにはいくらかかるでしょうか。
▶ **1** 20ドル。 **2** 40ドル。 **3** 45ドル。 **4** 100ドル。
Tickets: の部分に注目しましょう。大人は15ドル，8歳以下の子どもは5ドルです。

(2) 祭りに参加する人は～ことはできないでしょう。
▶ **1** アフリカ音楽の演奏を聞く
2 アフリカのダンスを見て楽しむ
3 アフリカの言語を話すのを学ぶ
4 アフリカの料理を試してみる
この祭りでできないことを選びます。**3**の内容はこの掲示に書いてありません。

PART 22

長文B

メール①

学習日

★理解度 □カンペキ! □もう一度 □まだまだ…

続いて「メール」文を読んでいきましょう。メールは1往復のものと1往復半のものがあります。

覚えよう
From:送信者
To:受信者
Date:日付
Subject:件名
はメールの最初につきます

先に設問を読もう いきなり長文を読み始めるのではなく，まずは設問を読み長文の内容をつかみましょう。

設問1 Why is Yuina nervous?
ユイナは（ なぜ ）緊張しているのですか。

選択肢
1 She cannot speak English at all. 英語がまったく話せないから。
2 She has to perform on the stage. 舞台で演じなくてはならないから。
3 She has never been outside of Japan. 日本の外に一度も行ったことがないから。
4 She is not good at swimming. 泳ぐことが得意ではないから。

解答（ 3 ）

設問2 Yuina started to study English
ユイナが英語を（ 勉強 ）し始めたのは

選択肢
1 at school. 学校で。
2 to watch musicals. ミュージカルを見るために。
3 to travel abroad. 海外旅行をするために。
4 five years ago. 5年前に。

解答（ 4 ）

設問3 What plan has Daisy's family made?
デイジーの家族は何の（ 計画 ）を立てましたか。

選択肢
1 Take Yuina to the sea. ユイナを海に連れていく。
2 Give Yuina English lessons. ユイナに英語のレッスンをする。
3 Hold a big festival. 大きなお祭りを開催する。
4 Buy a new jacket. 新しい上着を買う。

解答（ 1 ）

長文を読んでみよう 設問をふまえて，メール文を読んでいきましょう。

日本語訳

送信者：タナカ・ユイナ
受信者：デイジー・ニューマン
日付：6月14日
件名：日本からのごあいさつです!

親愛なるデイジー
こんにちは! ユイナです。7月に2週間，あなたの家に滞在する予定です。あなたとあなたの家族が，私のホストファミリーで私はうれしいです。私はカナダで勉強する機会を得て，とてもわくわくしています。海外旅行するのは今回が初めてなので，私は少々緊張しています。私は5年間英語を勉強していますが，いまだに話すことは得意ではありません。あなたが私の英語を理解してくれるといいのですが。私は学校で演劇部に入っています。私の夢はミュージカルの役者になって，国際的な舞台で演じることです。その理由で，私は英語がもっと得意になりたいです。私はあなたとたくさんの思い出を作ることも望んでいます。すぐに会えることを楽しみにしています。
心から
ユイナ

送信者：デイジー・ニューマン
受信者：タナカ・ユイナ
日付：6月14日
件名：待ちきれないわ!

こんにちは，ユイナ
どうか緊張しないで。私たちは一緒にすばらしい時間を過ごすのよ。私には兄弟も姉妹もいないから，あなたのホストシスターになれて幸せよ。あなたが明確な目標を持って，最善を尽くしてみることはすばらしいわ。あなたの夢がかなうことを願っています。実は，私たちの市はあなたにぴったりなの! あなたの滞在中に，舞台芸術を楽しむ大きなお祭りがここで開催されるの。毎年，世界中の多くの人がショーを見に来ます。あなたはきっと楽しいと思うわ! ここでは夜と昼の気温がとても違うので，上着が必要よ。それと，水着を持ってくるのを忘れないで。私たちはあなたを海に連れていくことを計画しているの。質問を何でも私に送ってね。
あなたの新しいお姉さん，
デイジー

練習問題

***(1)* 2 *(2)* 3 *(3)* 1**

解説

日本語訳

送信者：リンダ・マクドナルド
受信者：キャロライン・マクドナルド
日付：10月27日
件名：興味ある?

おはよう!
毎日朝食をとっている? 朝食は大切なのよ。最近は，パパと私は毎日新鮮な牛乳を飲んでいます。それぞれの家庭に牛乳を配達する会社があるの。その会社は自前の農場を持っていて，高品質の食べ物を牛に与えているから，彼らの牛乳は安全で健康的なの。それと，返却して再利用するガラスびんで来るから環境にも優しいの。彼らは週に2回配達するわ。スーパーマーケットの牛乳よりも高いけど，ずっとおいしいわよ! ひとつ試してみない?
愛をこめて
ママ

送信者：キャロライン・マクドナルド
受信者：リンダ・マクドナルド
日付：10月28日
件名：こういうのはどう?

こんにちは，ママ
それはおもしろそうね! もっとそれについて知るために，彼らのウェブサイトを訪れたわ。ミルク以外に，アイスクリーム，バター，ヨーグルトや3種類のチーズを注文できるのね。アイスクリームを試したいけど，いくつか問題があるの。私は日中たいてい家にいなくて，郵便受けはアイスクリームや他のものを保管するのによい場所ではないの。なので，考えがあるわ。自分の注文をあなたの家に届けるように頼むつもり。私のをあなたの注文と一緒に冷たく保つように頼んでもいいかしら。1週間に2回会社からの帰り道に立ち寄って，私の注文を受け取って家に持っていくわ。ときどき一緒に夕食をとるのも私たちにとってよいと思うの。どう思う?
ハグを
キャロライン

(1) その牛乳は何が特別なのですか。
▶ **1** 市場価格より安い。 **2** 環境に良い。
3 手に入れやすい。 **4** 冷やしておく必要がない。
リンダのメールの中に，it's eco-friendlyとあります。

(2) その会社に注文できない食べ物類は何ですか。
▶ **1** 牛乳とチーズ。 **2** ヨーグルトとアイスクリーム。
3 肉と魚。 **4** バターとチーズ。
質問文のcannot be orderedに注意しましょう。注文できないものを選びます。

(3) キャロラインは，なぜ自分の注文をリンダの家に配達してほしいのですか。
▶ **1** 注文が到着するとき彼女はいないから。
2 彼女のマンションの建物は郵便受けがないから。
3 その会社はキャロラインの地域には配達しないから。
4 リンダの家は，より彼女の会社に近いから。
キャロラインのメールの中の，I'm usually not at home during the daytime, ～.の文に注目します。

PART 23

長文B

メール②

学習日

★理解度
□カンペキ!
□もう一度
□まだまだ…

「メール」文を読んでいきましょう。

先に設問を読もう いきなり長文を読み始めるのではなく，まずは設問を読み長文の内容をつかみましょう。

設問1 What aren't the girls going to do at the party?

女の子たちは（ パーティー ）で何をしないつもりですか。

選択肢
1 Eat lots of snacks. お菓子をたくさん食べること。
2 Play video games. テレビゲームをすること。
3 Watch several movies. いくつかの映画を見ること。
4 Sleep for hours. 何時間も寝ること。

解答（ 4 ）

設問2 Amelia asks Erica to eat dinner with her family because

アメリアはエリカに自分の家族と一緒に（ 夕食 ）をとるように頼みました。なぜなら

選択肢
1 Erica needs to arrive early. エリカが早く到着する必要があるから。
2 Erica has to go home by seven. エリカは7時までに帰宅しなくてはならないから。
3 Erica doesn't like snacks. エリカはお菓子が好きではないから。
4 They want to talk before the others arrive. 彼女たちは他の人たちが来る前に話したいから。

解答（ 1 ）

設問3 Why was Samantha invited?

サマンサはなぜ（ 招待 ）されたのですか。

選択肢
1 She is in Erica's art class. 彼女がエリカの美術のクラスにいるから。
2 Her mother works at night. 彼女の母親が夜働いているから。
3 She is going to invite Lizzy. 彼女はリジーを招待するつもりだから。
4 Lizzy wasn't able to come. リジーが来ることができなかったから。

解答（ 4 ）

覚えよう

Subject（件名）は，メール文を読むためのヒントになります

長文を読んでみよう 設問をふまえて，メール文を読んでいきましょう。

日本語訳

送信者：アメリア・ジェンセン
受信者：エリカ・ゴンザレス
日付：6月14日
件名：私の家でのパーティー

こんにちは，エリカ
私は学校が終わってとてもうれしいわ！ 私の成績が良かったから，パーティーをしてお祝いしてもいいと両親が言うのよ。私は4人の女の子をオールナイトパーティーに招待することができるの。私たちは眠らずにお話をしたり音楽を聞いたりして楽しむことができると思うの。あなたはどう思う？ パーティーは晩の7時に始まって，朝の10時に終わることになると思うの。あなたはどの夜が良いかしら。次の金曜日？ それとも土曜日？ 私に教えてね。
アメリア

送信者：エリカ・ゴンザレス
受信者：アメリア・ジェンセン
日付：6月14日
件名：わくわくしそうね！

こんにちは，アメリア
それはすばらしいわ！ どちらかの夜は大丈夫だと思うわ。自分のコンピューターを持っていくつもり。私たちがプレイできるたくさんのゲームを持っているの。6時半に到着してもいいかしら。私のお母さんがあなたの家に送ってくれる予定なの。彼女は週末は7時までに職場にいないといけないから。他はだれを招待しているの？
またね。
エリカ

送信者：アメリア・ジェンセン
受信者：エリカ・ゴンザレス
日付：6月14日
件名：土曜日のパーティー

こんにちは，エリカ
もちろん，あなたは6時半に着いてもいいわよ！ もっと早く来て，私と私の家族と一緒に夕食を食べるのはどうかしら。私はリジーが来るといいと思っていたんだけど，彼女は週末中，町の外にいる予定なの。私は代わりに美術のクラスからサマンサを招待したわ。パーティーは，カーソンとジュリアとサマンサが都合がいいので土曜日に行われる予定よ。彼女たちは音楽と映画を持ってくるわ。母は私たち5人のためにたくさんのお菓子を作る予定。一晩中楽しみましょう！
あなたの親友
アメリア

練習問題

(1) 1　(2) 1　(3) 3

解説

日本語訳

送信者：ライアン・シルバー
受信者：ハラダ・ケイタ
日付：3月30日
件名：元気かい？

こんにちは，ケイタ
君が僕の家を離れてから2週間がたったね。日本人の兄弟ができたことはとても楽しかったよ。日本の新年度の開始前に君が帰らなくてはならなかったことは理解しているんだけれど，とてもさみしいよ！　君がアメリカの学校の6月の学年末にいないことは残念だよ。僕に君のそろばんをくれてありがとう。とても気に入ったよ。使い方を教えてくれないかな。君は暗算がとても得意だよね。僕はそれができるようになりたいよ。僕に秘密を教えて！
君の友達
ライアン

送信者：ハラダ・ケイタ
受信者：ライアン・シルバー
日付：4月1日
件名：どういたしまして

こんにちは，ライアン
僕も君がいなくてさみしいよ。君の家族やアメリカの友達すべてもね。君は僕がアメリカに滞在している間，とても親切だったね。さて，僕は日本の自分の生活に戻るためにいくつかの困難を抱えているよ。僕はときどき，もう自分がアメリカにいないことを忘れるんだ。昨日，自宅に入るとき，くつをぬぐのをほとんど忘れかけたよ。君がそろばんを気に入ってうれしいよ。それをとても上手に使うには，君は何らかの練習が必要だ。日本の子どもたちは，学校でその使い方を習うよ。ファイルを君にメールするね。それには暗算がうまくなるためにどのようにそろばんを使うかが書いてあるよ。
君の日本の兄弟
ケイタ

送信者：ライアン・シルバー
受信者：ハラダ・ケイタ
日付：4月1日
件名：すばらしい！

こんにちは，ケイタ
ファイルを送ってくれてありがとう。数学のクラスの友達のティムとジェニーもそろばんに興味を持っているよ。今僕たち全員は，ファイルを読んで学ぼうとしているところだよ。少しずつそろばんを使うのが上手になると思うよ。どんな感じかまた知らせるね。
ありがとう。
ライアン

(1) ライアンとケイタはなぜ知り合いなのですか。

▶ **1** ケイタはライアンの家族のところに滞在したから。
2 ティムとジェニーがライアンをケイタに紹介したから。
3 ライアンは日本で交換留学生だったから。
4 ケイタはライアンの数学の先生だったから。

ライアンのメールの最初の2文などから，ケイタがライアンの家にホームステイしていたことがわかります。

(2) ライアンは何の手伝いが必要ですか。

▶ **1** 数学のための日本の道具を使うこと。
2 日本の慣習に従うこと。
3 日本の文字を書くことを学ぶこと。
4 メールでファイルを送ること。

ライアンからの1つ目のメールのThanks for giving me your *soroban.* などから，このメールのやりとりで，そろばんのことが話題になっていることをつかみましょう。

(3) ライアンとティムとジェニーは一緒に何をしていますか。

▶ **1** 数学の試験を受けている。
2 数学の問題を作っている。
3 そろばんの使い方を学んでいる。
4 数学の授業で子どもたちに教えている。

ライアンからの2つ目のメールにあるTim and Jenny, ～. Now we're all trying to learn ～. などの文に注目しましょう。

PART 24

長文C

説明文①

学習日 ／

★理解度
□カンペキ!
□もう一度
□まだまだ…

先に設問を読もう 最後に「説明文」を読んでいきます。まずは設問を読み長文の内容をつかみましょう。

覚えよう
段落ごとに内容をつかもう

設問1 How were the Lascaux Cave paintings discovered?
ラスコー洞窟の壁画は，どのように（ 発見 ）されましたか。

選択肢
1 Dr. Rappenglueck was looking for old star maps. ラッペングレック博士が古い星図を探していた。
2 Some people went into the cave for hunting. 何人かの人々が狩猟で洞窟に入った。
3 A dog fell into a hole and its owner looked for him. 犬が穴に落ちて，飼い主が彼を探した。
4 Four French teenagers went out for a walk. 4人のフランスの10代が散歩に出かけた。

解答（ 3 ）

設問2 When were the drawings made?
壁画は（ いつ ）作られましたか。

選択肢
1 At least 15,000 years ago. 少なくとも1万5,000年前。
2 In 1963. 1963年。
3 More than 17,000 years ago. 1万7,000年以上前。
4 Less than eighty years ago. 80年前未満。

解答（ 1 ）

設問3 What happened in 1963?
1963年に（ 何 ）が起きましたか。

選択肢
1 A cave with paintings was opened to visitors. 壁画がある洞窟が，訪問者に開放された。
2 A German scientist found the oldest star map in the cave. あるドイツ人の科学者が，洞窟で最古の星図を見つけた。
3 Damage to the paintings led to closing the cave to visitors. 壁画へのダメージによって，訪問者に洞窟が閉じられた。
4 Four boys happened to find old paintings in a cave. 4人の少年が，洞窟でたまたま古い壁画を見つけた。

解答（ 3 ）

覚えよう

設問4 What is this story about?
この話は何についてですか。

選択肢
1 The adventures of Marcel and his dog Robot. マーセルと彼の犬，ロボットの冒険。
2 A cave with very old paintings studied by scientists. 科学者たちによって研究されたとても古い壁画がある洞窟。
3 How maps in a cave were saved. 洞窟の地図はどのように保存されたか。
4 The danger to teenagers going into caves. 洞窟に入る10代にとっての危険。

解答（ 2 ）

長文を読んでみよう 設問をふまえて，説明文を読んでいきましょう。

日本語訳

最古の星図

80年以上前，10代のフランス人であるマーセルはロボットという犬と一緒に散歩に出かけました。突然その犬が，地面の小さな穴に落ちました。マーセルは走って3人の友達を呼び，ろうそくを手にしてロボットを探しに行きました。彼らが見つけたのは，洞窟の壁にある何百もの動物の壁画と，ロボットでした。

壁画を研究していた科学者たちは，それらは1万5000年前から1万7000年前の間に作られたと突き止めました。とてもすばらしい馬，シカ，猫や他の動物たちの壁画がありました。それらのいくつかは今は絶滅したか想像上のものです。鳥の首をした男の人を見ることもできます。彼らは，その洞窟は長い間狩猟の成功のために祈るための儀式に使われたと考えました。

ラスコー洞窟とそのすばらしい壁画は，すぐに有名になり，多くの人がそれらを見に来ました。壁画はあまりに多くの訪問者に触れられたので，状態がすぐに悪くなりました。訪問者の息の中の二酸化炭素が壁画にダメージを与えもしました。1963年に洞窟は閉じられました。数人の科学者だけが，毎年その中に入ることができます。

それらの科学者のひとりであるラッペングレック博士という名のドイツ人は，壁画のうちの2，3はもっとも古い星図のひとつだと今は考えています。彼は，ひとつの星図はベガやデネブやアルタイルの星が1万6500年前にどこにあったかを示していると考えています。別の壁画は，プレアデス星団が昔どこにあったかを表しているかもしれません。マーセルが発見したラスコー洞窟を訪れることはできませんが，近くの洞窟に壁画の複製があります。何千もの訪問者が，毎年それらを見にやってきます。おそらくいつかあなたもそこへ行くことでしょう。

練習問題

(1) 3　(2) 1　(3) 2　(4) 4　(5) 2

解説

日本語訳

クリーンエネルギーのための計画

気候変動は，私たちが抱える最も大きな問題の１つです。科学者たちはそれを長い間ずっと心配しています。気候変動のために，より大きな嵐，大規模な森林火災や洪水が世界中で起こっています。科学者たちは増えつつある二酸化炭素排出量が気候変動を引き起こしていると考えています。地球の二酸化炭素排出量の大半は化石燃料からです。今，私たちはクリーンエネルギーを使うことを考えるべきです。ひとつの例が太陽光発電です。

アメリカのエネルギー省（DOE）は最近，化石燃料を使うことをやめる計画について話しました。アメリカ合衆国は2035年までに100%クリーンな電気を使う計画をしています。太陽光発電は，その計画の重要な部分です。彼らはより低い費用で太陽光発電を生産したいと思っています。彼らの目標は，次の10年で太陽光発電の費用を60%削減することです。

目標に達するために，DOEは１億2800万ドル以上を費やす予定です。彼らは太陽光発電の技術を改善することが必要だと考えています。彼らはまた，よりよい発電所と電力の供給の方法のためにお金を払おうとしています。

一方で，その計画を好ましく思わない人々もいます。目標はあまりにも難しいので，そんなに早く達成できないと言う人がいます。計画にはあまりに多くのお金が必要なので，費用は使用者でまかなわれるだろうと言う人もいます。彼らの考えでは，人々は太陽光電気のためにもっとお金を払い続けることになるでしょう。また，化石燃料は常に必要とされ続けるだろうといまだに感じる人もいます。DOEは成功のためには，それに達する強い目標とお金が必要だと言っています。

(1) 科学者たちは何をずっと心配していますか。

▶ **1** 大規模な森林火災。　**2** 洪水。
3 気候変動。　**4** 海洋の温度。
本文の最初の文に注目します。Climate change is ～. とあります。

(2) アメリカ合衆国のエネルギー省の目標は

▶ **1** 太陽光電気の費用を60%削減することです。
2 1億2800万ドル以上を費やすことだった。
3 化石燃料をよりよくすることです。
4 大規模な森林火災を止めることです。
第2段落の最後の文に注目します。to cut 以下がTheir goalの内容です。

(3) アメリカ合衆国は，クリーンな電気のみを使うことをいつに計画していますか。

▶ **1** 2020年以前。　**2** 2035年までに。
3 2030年のあとで。　**4** 2025年までに。
第2段落2文目に注目します。by 2035とあります。

(4) DOEの計画に賛成していない人もいます。なぜなら，

▶ **1** 気候変動は大きな問題ではないから。
2 10年の期間は長すぎるから。
3 別のクリーンなエネルギーがあるから。
4 その計画を実現するのは簡単ではないから。
最後の段落に，計画を好まない人たちの理由などが書かれています。

(5) この話は何についてですか。

▶ **1** エネルギー省の汚染。
2 太陽光電気をより安くすること。
3 気候変動の問題。
4 電気費用の高騰。
気候変動のことについても述べられていますが，英文全体は太陽光発電の費用に関することであることを把握しましょう。

PART 25

長文C

説明文②

学習日

★理解度 □カンペキ! □もう一度 □まだまだ…

先に設問を読もう 「説明文」を読んでいきます。まずは設問を読み長文の内容をつかみましょう。

覚えよう 段落ごとのまとまりで内容を整理しながら読みます

設問1 March Madness

マーチマッドネスは

選択肢
1 takes place once every four years. 4年ごとに行われます。
2 is the best basketball team in the U.S. アメリカで一番のバスケットボールチームです。
3 is a university sports tournament. 大学のスポーツトーナメントです。
4 starts on the first Sunday in March. 3月の第一日曜日に始まります。

解答(3)

設問2 March Madness is popular because

マーチマッドネスは(人気)があります。なぜなら

選択肢
1 the games are usually very exciting. 試合がたいていとてもわくわくするから。
2 basketball players are so tall. バスケットボールの選手がとても背が高いから。
3 so many people go to the games. とても多くの人が試合に行くから。
4 the games are held in universities. 試合が大学で開催されるから。

解答(1)

設問3 People can take part in the Bracket Challenge by

人々が勝ち上がり予想に(参加)することができるのは

選択肢
1 playing university basketball. 大学バスケットボールをすることによって。
2 paying a small amount of money. 少額のお金を支払って。
3 listening to a committee. 委員会を傍聴して。
4 writing the names of winning teams. 勝利チームの名前を書いて。

解答(4)

設問4 Why is it difficult to win the Bracket Challenge?

勝ち上がり予想に勝つのが(難しい)のはなぜですか。

選択肢
1 Basketball tournaments are difficult to win. バスケットボールのトーナメントは勝つのが難しいから。
2 Too many people join the game each year. 毎年あまりに多くの人々が試合に参加するから。
3 There are too many possible answers. 起こりうる答えがあまりにも多いから。
4 The game is controlled by the committee. 委員会によって試合が支配されているから。

解答(3)

長文を読んでみよう 設問をふまえて,説明文を読んでいきましょう。

日本語訳

マーチマッドネス

3月中,全米の多くの人々がスポーツトーナメントに興奮します。それは全米で男子の大学バスケットボールチームのナンバーワンを決めます。ベスト68のチームがお互いに競います。ほとんどのアメリカ人が,たとえ見ないとしてもこれらの試合について話します。そのトーナメントは「マーチマッドネス」と呼ばれています。

マーチマッドネスはとても人気があります。理由のひとつは,試合そのものがたいていとてもわくわくするものだからです。それらの多くが延長に突入することがふつうです。ときには最後の10秒でとてもすばらしいシュートが試合をひっくり返します。

どのチームが勝つかを予想して楽しめるのがもうひとつの理由です。それが「マーチマッドネス勝ち上がり予想ゲーム」です。たとえバスケットボールファンでなくても,全員がそれに参加することができます。3月中旬の日曜日に,委員会がどの68チームがトーナメントに参加できるかを発表します。同日に,委員会はオンライントーナメント表を提示します。あなたはどのチームがそれぞれの試合で勝つかを予想し,トーナメント表に彼らの名前を書きます。無料でゲームに参加することができ,勝者は100万ドルを受け取ります。

不運にも,今までにだれも賞金を手にしたことはありません。なぜか? なぜならトーナメントでは多くの試合があり,すべての試合を当てるのはほとんど不可能だからです。また,それらは想像を超えるドラマに満ちているからです。そのような理由で,人々はマーチマッドネスに夢中になるのです。

練習問題

(1) 3 **(2)** 4 **(3)** 1 **(4)** 3 **(5)** 2

解説

日本語訳

アメリカの桜の季節

日本では,尾崎行雄は「立憲政治の父」として知られていますが,アメリカ合衆国では彼は別の理由で有名です。東京の市長だったとき,尾崎は日本の吉野桜の木を3000本,2国間の友好の象徴としてアメリカ合衆国へ送りました。その木々は1912年にワシントンD.C.のポトマック川沿いに植えられ,多くの人々に愛されています。

毎年春に,全米桜祭りが3月と4月の約3週間そこで開催されます。祭りは1927年に始まりました。今,世界中の150万の人々が美しい桜を見に毎年来ます。

最初の3000本の木のうち約50本がまだ生きています。それらは109歳で,春にはいまだに美しい花を見せてくれます。吉野桜が50年以上生きるのは珍しいことです。これらの木は手厚く扱われています。それらの1本が枯れると,新たな木が引き継ぎます。それはしばしばファーストレディ,つまりアメリカの大統領の妻によって植えられます。例えば,2012年にはミシェル・オバマが植えました。

ワシントンD.C.のものが最も有名な一方で,アメリカ合衆国の別の場所も自分たちの桜の季節を祝います。例えば,人々は,国の真ん中のウィスコンシン州のドア郡に何千もの桜の木を見にやってきます。彼らの桜の季節は5月の中頃にやってきます。太平洋に近いオレゴン州のポートランドでは,100本の曙桜があるジャパニーズアメリカン・ヒストリカルプラザがあります。人々はたいてい3月中頃に桜を楽しみます。

(1) 尾崎行雄はアメリカでなぜ有名なのですか。

▸ **1** 政府を打ち立てることを助けたから。
2 アメリカ大統領の妻に親切だったから。
3 アメリカにあげた贈り物のため。
4 最初のアメリカの桜祭りを始めたから。

本文2行目の,When he was ～で始まる文に注目します。

(2) 全米桜祭りは

▸ **1** 1912年に始まりました。
2 5月中頃に開催されます。
3 1週間続きます。
4 ワシントンD.C.で開催されます。

第2段落の最初の文に注目します。is held thereのthereは前の段落で出てきたWashington D.C.のことです。選択肢ではis heldがtakes placeと言い換えら

れています。

(3) 吉野桜はたいてい

▶ **1** 50年以下しか生きません。

2 花の生産をやめるまで生きます。

3 100年以上生きます。

4 引き抜かれるまで生きます。

第3段落のIt's rare for Yoshino cherry trees to live ～. に注目します。

(4) 4つの市のうちで，1年の最後に桜の季節が来るのはどこですか。

▶ **1** 東京。　**2** ワシントンD.C.。

3 ドア郡。　**4** ポートランド。

ドア郡では，桜の季節はin mid-Mayとあります。

(5) この話は何についてですか。

▶ **1** 桜の木を植える人。

2 アメリカでどれだけ桜が愛されているか。

3 桜の木がどのくらい長く生きることができるか。

4 日本とアメリカの人々の友情。

英文全体として何が書かれているかを読み取りましょう。

PART 26 英作文①Eメール
形式の注意点

学習日

★理解度
□カンペキ!
□もう一度
□まだまだ…

ライティング（英作文）では「Eメール」を書く問題が出題されます。

ルールを押さえよう 「Eメール」の問題でのルールを確認しましょう。

・「2つの質問」に答えること　・「15~25語で」書くこと
・相手のEメールに対応した内容であること

注意! 内容・語彙・文法の3つの観点で採点されます。各観点4点で，12点満点です。なお，カンマ(,)やピリオド(.)は語数には含めません

質問に使われる表現 Eメールに書かれた質問の内容を理解するために，質問でよく使われる表現を確認しましょう。

「何?」　(What) kind of food do you like? (あなたが好きな食べ物の種類は何ですか)
「だれ?」　(Who) do you respect? (あなたはだれを尊敬していますか)
「どこ?」　(Where) did you go last winter? (あなたはこの前の冬にどこに行きましたか)
「どのような?」　(How) was your vacation? (あなたの休暇はどうでしたか)
「いくつ?」　How (many) classes were there? (クラスの数はいくつでしたか)

「いつ~?」	When ~?	「なぜ~?」	Why ~?	「どっち~?」	Which ~?

質問への返答に使える表現 質問に対する返答を書く際に使える表現を確認しましょう。

I like ~	私は~〈物など〉が好きです	I went to ~	私は~〈場所〉へ行きました
I respect ~	私は~〈人物〉を尊敬しています	It's because ~	~〈理由〉だからです
My birthday is ~	私の誕生日は~〈時〉です	It was ~	~〈様子〉でした

冒頭文を書く 返信メールでは，いきなり質問に答えるのではなく，まずは相手のEメールの内容に対応した冒頭文を書きましょう。

That's wonderful! (それはすてきですね)
I'm (studying) hard every day. (私は毎日一生懸命に勉強をしています)
I (had) a great summer vacation. (私の夏休みはすばらしかったです)

締めくくりの文を書く 最後に，締めくくりの文を書きましょう。

I'm really excited about the trip. (私は旅行が本当に楽しみです)
I will do my (best) for the test. (私はテストのためにベストを尽くします)
I hope to see you (someday). (いつかあなたに会えることを願っています)

覚えよう 語数調整をしながら文をふくらませましょう

練習問題

Hi,

How are you doing?
You told me that you are going on vacation next week. I went to Hawaii with my family last weekend. Where will you go? Also, what will you do there? Please tell me about it!

Your friend,
Laurie

Eメール訳
こんにちは,
調子はどうですか。
あなたは来週休みだと私に教えてくれましたね。私は先週末に家族とハワイに行きました。あなたはどこへ行きますか。それと，そこで何をしますか。それについて私に教えてください!
あなたの友達,
ローリー

Hi, Laurie!

Thank you for your e-mail.
Did you enjoy (Hawaii)? I'll (go) to Yamanashi (next) week. I'll (enjoy) the beautiful (view) of Mt. Fuji! I have (never) been there before.

Best wishes,

《 enjoy　go　next　Hawaii　never　view 》

返信メール訳
こんにちは，ローリー!
Eメールをありがとう。
あなたはハワイを楽しみましたか。私は来週，山梨へ行きます。私は富士山の美しい眺めを楽しみます! 私はそこに一度も行ったことがありません。
幸せを願って

PART 27

英作文②Eメール

実践

学習日 ／

★理解度
□カンペキ!
□もう一度
□まだまだ…

本番の形式に近い形でEメールの返信を書いてみましょう。

> Hello,
>
> Thanks for writing me.
> You wrote that you went camping last weekend. I want to hear all about it! Who did you go with? How was the weather? I'm going camping soon, too.
>
> Your friend,
> Mark

冒頭文を書こう まずは，Eメールの内容を受けた冒頭文を書きましょう。

You wrote that you went camping last weekend.に対して
あなたは先週末キャンプに行ったと書いていました

はい，その通りです。	はい，私はキャンプに行きました。
Yes, (that's) right.	Yes, I (went) camping.

I'm going camping soon, too.に対して
私も近々，キャンプに行きます

わあ，それはすばらしいですね。
Oh, (that's) great.

2つの質問に答えよう 質問の内容を確認し，それに対する答えを書きましょう。

Who did you go with? あなたはだれと行きましたか

私は家族とキャンプに行きました。
I went camping (with) my (family).

How was the weather? 天気はどうでしたか

晴れて暖かかったです。
(It) was (sunny) and warm.

締めくくりの文を書く 最後に締めくくりの文を書きましょう。

また行けるといいと思います。	次は一緒に行きましょう。
I (hope) we can go again.	(Let's) go together next time.

練習問題

> Hi,
>
> I went to your house today, but you weren't at home. Where did you go? Also, what did you do there? I am free all weekend. Let's do something together tomorrow!
>
> Your friend,
> Josh

Eメール訳

こんにちは，
私は今日あなたの家に行きましたが，あなたは留守でした。
あなたはどこへ行きましたか。それと，そこで何をしましたか。
私は週末ずっと暇です。明日一緒に何かしましょう！
あなたの友達，
ジョシュ

Hi, Josh!
こんにちは，ジョシュ！

Thank you for your e-mail.
Eメールをありがとう。

(解答例1)

I was busy today. I went to the beach with my family. I swam in the sea all day. Let's go shopping tomorrow.

(23語)

(解答例2)

Sorry, I wasn't at home. I went to the shopping mall. I bought some new stationery for school. Let's go to the movies together tomorrow. (25語)

Kind regards,
敬具

解答例1訳

今日は忙しかったです。私は家族と海岸に行きました。私は一日中海で泳ぎました。明日は買い物に行きましょう。

解答例2訳

ごめんなさい，私は家にいませんでした。私はショッピングモールに行きました。私は学校用の新しい文房具をいくつか買いました。明日は一緒に映画に行きましょう。

PART 28

英作文③意見論述

形式の注意点

学習日

★理解度
□カンペキ!
□もう一度
□まだまだ…

ライティング2問目では,「外国人の友達から質問された」という設定でQUESTIONが出題されます。

ルールを押さえよう 意見論述の問題では,守らないと減点になったり,採点の対象外になったりするルールがあります。

・「意見とその理由を2つ」書くこと
・「25~35語で」書くこと
・QUESTIONに対応した内容であること

注意! カンマ(,)やピリオド(.)は語数には含めません

解答文の基本の構成を理解しよう

解答文を書くとき,書き方のフォーマットを知っていると便利です。

賛成・反対の表明	賛成の場合 I think that ~ (~と思います) 反対の場合 I don't think ~ (~とは思いません)
理由①	First, ~ (第一に,~)
理由②	Second, ~ (第二に,~)

覚えよう さまざまな表現を覚えておくと,語数の調整にも使えます

使える表現 他にも使える表現を覚えておきましょう。

I think (that) ~	~と思います	I agree (that) ~	~ということに賛成です
I don't think (that) ~	~とは思いません	I don't agree (that) ~	~ということには賛成しません
I disagree (that) ~	~ということには反対です	My favorite ~ is ...	私が大好きな~は…です

first	第一に	first of all	まず第一に
second	第二に	also	また
for example	例えば	such as	~のような
in addition	さらには	moreover	そのうえ
not only that	それだけでなく	on the other hand	その一方で
in spite of that	それにもかかわらず	because of this	このため
in my opinion	私の 意見 では	for these reasons	これらの 理由 により
therefore	したがって	that's why ~	それが~の理由です

練習問題

次の( )に入れるのに適切な語句を,[ ]から選んで書き入れましょう。ただし先頭にくる語も小文字になっています。

● あなたは,外国人の友達から以下のQUESTIONをされました。
● QUESTIONについて,あなたの意見とその理由を2つ英文で書きなさい。
● 語数の目安は25語~35語です。

QUESTION: ***Which do you like better, dogs or cats?***
質問:あなたは犬と猫のどちらがより好きですか。

犬のほうが好きな場合

I (like) dogs better. I (have) two (reasons). (First), dogs are smart, so some dogs work for the police. (Second), I can walk and play outside with them. It is good for my health.

[first like reasons second have]

私は犬のほうが好きです。理由は2つあります。第一に,犬は賢いです。だから,警察のために働く犬もいます。第二に,彼らと一緒に散歩したり外で遊んだりすることができます。それは健康にとって良いです。

猫のほうが好きな場合

I (like) cats better. I (have two reasons). (First), cats don't bark loudly, (so) they aren't noisy in my room. (Second), I don't have to take them for a walk. Keeping them isn't hard.

[first like so second have two reasons]

私は猫のほうが好きです。理由は2つあります。第一に,猫は大声でほえません。だから,部屋の中で騒がしくありません。二番目に,彼らを散歩に連れていく必要がありません。彼らを飼うことは大変ではありません。

PART 29

英作文④意見論述

ブレインストーミング

学習日

★理解度
□カンペキ!
□もう一度
□まだまだ…

意見論述の問題では,いきなり答えを書き始めるのではなく,質問を見て答えの候補を挙げていくと書きやすくなります。

QUESTION: ***What subject do you like studying the best?***
質問:あなたはどの教科を勉強することが一番好きですか。

理科が好きな場合

I like studying science the best.
私は理科を勉強することが一番好きです。

その理由をいくつか挙げよう

・動物や植物について学ぶことが好き。
I like learning (about) animals and plants.
・理科の授業は楽しい。
(Science) classes are fun.
・理科は日常生活に役立つ。
Science is (useful) for everyday life.
・将来エンジニアになりたいので,もっと理科を勉強したい。
I want to be an (engineer) in the future, so I want to study science more.

注意! 理由は,まったく違うことについて書きます。同じような内容だと減点されてしまいます

英語が好きな場合

I like studying English the best.
私は英語を勉強することが一番好きです。

その理由をいくつか挙げよう

・英語で映画を楽しみたい。
I want to (enjoy) many movies in English.
・外国の友達を作りたい。
I want to make a lot of friends from (foreign) countries.
・さまざまな文化を学ぶことは興味深い。
Learning different cultures is (interesting).
・海外旅行で役に立つ。
English is useful when I (travel) abroad.

練習問題

QUESTION: ***Which do you like better, eating out or at home?***
質問:外食と家で食べるのでは,どちらが好きですか。

上の質問について,好きな理由を日本語でそれぞれ4つずつ書きましょう。できるだけ簡単な日本語で書くのがコツです。

外食が好きな場合

・(例)家族以外の人との食事を楽しめる。
・いろいろなメニューから選べる。
・家族のだれかが料理をしなくてすむ。
・後片付けをする必要がない。
・プロの料理人の味を楽しめる。

家で食べるのが好きな場合

・(例)時間を気にしなくてよい。
・食費を節約できる。
・リラックスして食事ができる。
・食材を自分で選ぶことができる。
・自分で料理をすることが好き。

上で書いた理由のうち,英語にできそうなものをそれぞれ2つずつ選び,英語で書きましょう。

外食が好きな場合

・I can choose different kinds of foods.
・We don't have to clean up the dishes.

家で食べるのが好きな場合

・I can save money on food.
・I can relax when I eat at home.

PART 30

英作文⑤意見論述

和文英訳

学習日

★理解度
□カンペキ!
□もう一度
□まだまだ…

本番の形式に近い形で練習していきましょう。

QUESTION: *Do you often go to the library?*

質問：あなたは（ 図書館 ）によく行きますか。

上の質問について，あなたの意見とその理由２つを日本語で書きましょう。

(はい)・いいえ
私は図書館に（ よく行きます ）。
理由は２つあります。
１つ目は（ 興味のある本が，無料でたくさん読むことができる ）からです。
２つ目は（ 勉強する場所としても最適だ ）からです。

上で書いた日本語を英訳しましょう。

I often go to the library.
I have two reasons.
First, I can read many interesting books for free.
Second, I think the library is the best place to study.

覚えよう
Do you ～?にはYesやNoで答えます

注意!
英訳しやすいように，かんたんな日本語で書くのがコツです

練習問題

質問：あなたはどの国を訪れたいですか。

（解答例1）（Australia）

I want to visit Australia because I'm interested in animals living there. For example I want to hold koalas. Also, I want to walk on a beautiful beach and swim in the sea. （33語）

解答例1訳　私はそこに生息する動物に興味があるので，オーストラリアを訪れたいです。例えばコアラを抱っこしたいです。また，美しい浜辺を歩いて海で泳ぎたいです。

（解答例2）（France）

I want to visit France. I have two reasons. First, I can enjoy delicious French food at a restaurant or a cafe. Second, I want to visit some museums and enjoy famous works of art. （35語）

解答例2訳　私はフランスを訪れたいです。理由は2つあります。第1に，レストランやカフェでおいしいフランス料理を楽しむことができます。第2に，博物館を訪れて有名な美術作品を楽しみたいです。

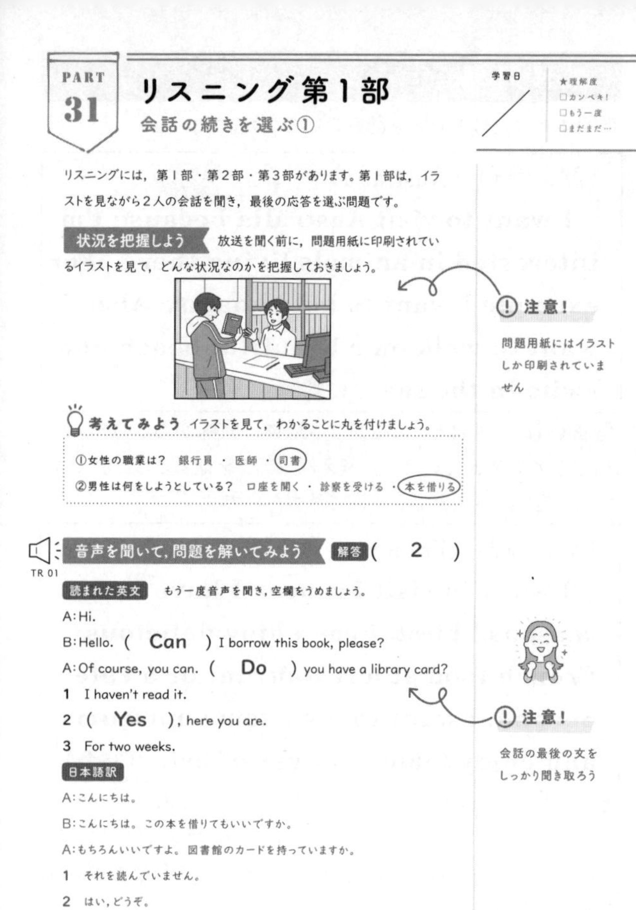
PART 31 リスニング第1部
会話の続きを選ぶ①

学習日

★理解度
□カンペキ!
□もう一度
□まだまだ…

リスニングには，第1部・第2部・第3部があります。第1部は，イラストを見ながら2人の会話を聞き，最後の応答を選ぶ問題です。

状況を把握しよう　放送文を聞く前に，問題用紙に印刷されているイラストを見て，どんな状況なのかを把握しておきましょう。

注意！
問題用紙にはイラストしか印刷されていません

考えてみよう　イラストを見て，わかることに丸を付けましょう。

①女性の職業は？　銀行員 ・ 医師 ・ (司書)

②男性は何をしようとしている？　口座を開く ・ 診察を受ける ・ (本を借りる)

TR 01
音声を聞いて，問題を解いてみよう　解答（　2　）

読まれた英文　もう一度音声を聞き，空欄をうめましょう。

A: Hi.

B: Hello. (　Can　) I borrow this book, please?

A: Of course, you can. (　Do　) you have a library card?

1　I haven't read it.

2　(　Yes　), here you are.

3　For two weeks.

注意！
会話の最後の文をしっかり聞き取ろう

日本語訳

A: こんにちは。

B: こんにちは。この本を借りてもいいですか。

A: もちろんいいですよ。図書館のカードを持っていますか。

1　それを読んでいません。

2　はい，どうぞ。

3　2週間です。

84

練習問題

(1) 1　**(2)** 2　**(3)** 1　**(4)** 3　**(5)** 1　**(6)** 2

解説

(1) 放送文　A: Hello. This is Mike Jones.

B: Hello. This is Thomas Trading Company. Can I help you?

A: Can I speak to Mr. Morgan?

1 Sorry, he's out now.

2 Yes, he's in a meeting now.

3 I can't speak to him.

日本語訳　A：もしもし。マイク・ジョーンズです。

B：もしもし。トーマス商事です。ご用件を承ります。

A：モーガンさんをお願いできますか。

▶ **1** 申し訳ございませんが，彼は外出中です。

2 はい，彼は今会議中です。

3 私は彼に話しかけることができません。

(2) 放送文　A: What are you going to do after school?

B: Well, I have no plans.

A: Why don't we go to see a movie?

1 OK. The movie was interesting.

2 Sounds nice.

3 Sorry, I have to go home today.

日本語訳　A：放課後は何をするつもり？

B：えーと，何も計画はないよ。

A：映画を見に行くのはどう？

▶ **1** わかったわ。その映画はおもしろかった。

2 いいわね。　**3** ごめん，今日は帰らなければならないの。

(3) 放送文　A: This coffee is very delicious.

B: Yeah. I bought it at the coffee shop in front of the station.

A: Really? Is it expensive?

1 Not very.

2 No, it is made in Hawaii.

3 No, I can't buy it again.

日本語訳　A：このコーヒーはとてもおいしいね。

B：ええ。駅前のコーヒー店でそれを買ったのよ。

A：本当に？　それは高いの？

▶ **1** そうでもないわ。　**2** いいえ，それはハワイ産よ。

3 いいえ，二度と買えないわ。

(4) 放送文　A: Have you finished making the report?

B: Yes, I've just finished it.

A: Good. Can I ask you to do some other work?

1 Sorry, I want to finish writing the report.

2 Yes, could you check my report?

3 Yes, what can I do?

日本語訳　A：報告書は作り終えましたか。

B：ええ，今終わったところです。

A：よかった。違う仕事を頼むことはできますか。

▶ **1** ごめんなさい，報告書を書き終えたいんです。

2 はい，報告書を確認してくださいますか。

3 はい，何をしましょうか。

(5) 放送文　A: What are we doing?

B: Do you like tennis? Let's have a game!

A: I like tennis, but I don't have a tennis racket to play with.

1 I have two rackets. I can lend you one.

2 I don't have a racket, either.

3 There is a tennis court here.

日本語訳　A：私たちは何をしようか。

B：あなたはテニスが好き？　試合をしましょう。

A：テニスは好きだけど，プレー用のテニスラケットを持ってないんだ。

▶ **1** 私が2本持っているわ。1本貸すわよ。

2 私もラケットを持っていないのよ。

3 ここにテニスコートがあるわ。

(6) 放送文　A: May I help you, sir?

B: Can you show me that jacket, please?

A: Which one do you mean?

1 I'm just looking.

2 The brown one.

3 I like it very much.

日本語訳　A：いらっしゃいませ，お客様。

B：あのジャケットを見せてくれますか。

A：どちらのものでしょうか。

▶ **1** 見ているだけです。　**2** 茶色いものです。

3 それがとても好きです。

PART 32

リスニング第1部

会話の続きを選ぶ②

学習日 ／

★理解度
□カンペキ!
□もう一度
□まだまだ…

第1部は，イラストを見ながら2人の会話を聞き，最後の応答を選ぶ問題です。問題用紙にはイラストしか印刷されていません。

状況を把握しよう 放送を聞く前に，問題用紙に印刷されているイラストを見て，どんな状況なのかを把握しておきましょう。

考えてみよう イラストを見て，わかることに丸を付けましょう。

①場所はどこ？（部屋の中）・ 学校の教室 ・ レストラン

②女性は何をしようとしている？

買い物をする ・ 授業を受ける ・（机を持ち上げる）

覚えよう

イラストの状況をイメージしながら音声を聞こう

TR 03

音声を聞いて，問題を解いてみよう 解答（ 1 ）

読まれた英文 もう一度音声を聞き，空欄をうめましょう。

A: Do you need any help?

B: Yes, please. This desk is too (heavy) for me.

A: No problem. (Where) do you want to move it?

1 Over there (by) the window.

2 Sorry, I'm busy now.

3 Thanks for helping me.

日本語訳

A：手伝おうか。

B：ええ，お願い。この机は私には重すぎるの。

A：問題ないよ。どこへ動かしたいの？

1 向こうの窓のそばに。

2 ごめんなさい，今は忙しいの。

3 手伝ってくれてありがとう。

86

練習問題

***(1)* 1 *(2)* 2 *(3)* 3 *(4)* 3 *(5)* 1 *(6)* 2**

解説

(1) **放送文** A: Can you help me?

B: Sure. What's the matter?

A: I cannot open this file.

1 How about restarting your computer?

2 Thank you very much.

3 Please write an e-mail to me.

日本語訳 A：助けてくれる？

B：いいわよ。どうしたの？

A：このファイルが開かないんだ。

▶ **1** コンピューターを再起動したらどうかしら。

2 どうもありがとう。 **3** 私にEメールを書いてね。

(2) **放送文** A: Excuse me. Does this bus go to the city museum?

B: No. Please take bus number 9.

A: Where is the bus stop?

1 Thanks a lot.

2 Over there.

3 It'll leave soon.

日本語訳 A：すみません，このバスは市立博物館に行きますか。

B：いいえ。9番のバスにお乗りください。

A：バス停はどこですか。

▶ **1** どうもありがとうございます。

2 あちらです。 **3** もうすぐ出発します。

(3) **放送文** A: What are you doing, Ken?

B: Mom, I'm going to take the dog for a walk.

A: Thanks, but have you done your homework?

1 I'll tell him that. **2** No, it was easy to do.

3 I have no homework today.

日本語訳 A：ケン，何をしているの？

B：ママ，犬を散歩に連れて行こうとしているんだ。

A：ありがとう，でも宿題はやったの？

▶ **1** 彼にそれを伝えるよ。

2 いいや，それはやるのは簡単だったよ。

3 今日は宿題がないんだ。

(4) **放送文** A: Hello, may I help you?

B: Can I have one hamburger and one small orange juice?

A: Sure. Anything else?

1 Thank you. **2** For here. **3** No, that's all.

日本語訳 A：こんにちは，いらっしゃいませ。

B：ハンバーガー1つとオレンジジュースのスモールを1つください。

A：わかりました。他には何かいかがですか。

▶ **1** ありがとう。 **2** ここで。 **3** いいえ，それで全部です。

(5) **放送文** A: What do you want to eat for dinner today?

B: I'd like to have chicken curry.

A: OK, but I have to get some chicken.

1 Shall I go and get it? **2** I don't like salad, either.

3 I'll help you make it.

日本語訳 A：今日の夕飯は何が食べたい？

B：チキンカレーが食べたいわ。

A：わかったよ，でもチキンを買ってこなくちゃ。

▶ **1** 私が行って買ってこようか？

2 私もサラダが好きではない。

3 あなたが作るのを手伝うわ。

(6) **放送文** A: I bought a new video game last week.

B: What kind of game?

A: A car racing game! Do you want to play it?

1 I like shooting games.

2 I'd love to.

3 I don't have a car.

日本語訳 A：先週新しいテレビゲームを買ったのよ。

B：どんなゲーム？

A：カーレースゲームよ！ やりたい？

▶ **1** 僕はシューティングゲームが好きなんだ。 **2** とっても。

3 車は持っていないよ。

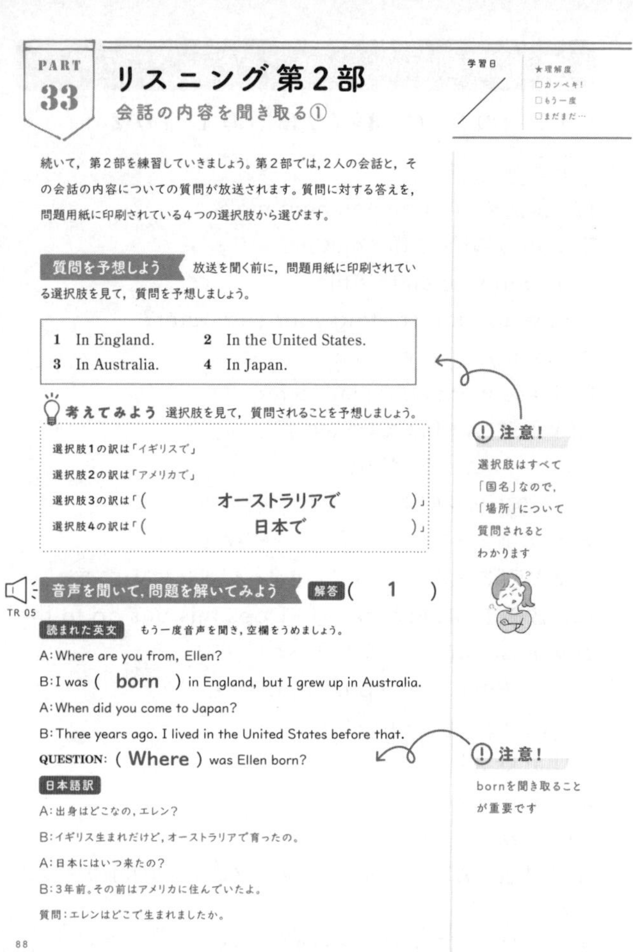

PART 33

リスニング第2部

会話の内容を聞き取る①

学習日 ★理解度 □カンペキ! □もう一度 □まだまだ…

続いて，第2部を練習していきましょう。第2部では，2人の会話と，その会話の内容についての質問が放送されます。質問に対する答えを，問題用紙に印刷されている4つの選択肢から選びます。

質問を予想しよう 放送を聞く前に，問題用紙に印刷されている選択肢を見て，質問を予想しましょう。

1	In England.	2	In the United States.
3	In Australia.	4	In Japan.

考えてみよう 選択肢を見て，質問されることを予想しましょう。

選択肢1の訳は「イギリスで」
選択肢2の訳は「アメリカで」
選択肢3の訳は「(オーストラリアで)」
選択肢4の訳は「(日本で)」

注意！ 選択肢はすべて「国名」なので，「場所」について質問されるとわかります

音声を聞いて，問題を解いてみよう 解答 (1)

TR 05

読まれた英文 もう一度音声を聞き，空欄をうめましょう。

A: Where are you from, Ellen?
B: I was (born) in England, but I grew up in Australia.
A: When did you come to Japan?
B: Three years ago. I lived in the United States before that.
QUESTION: (Where) was Ellen born?

注意！ bornを聞き取ることが重要です

日本語訳

A: 出身はどこなの，エレン?
B: イギリス生まれだけど，オーストラリアで育ったの。
A: 日本にはいつ来たの?
B: 3年前。その前はアメリカに住んでいたよ。
質問: エレンはどこで生まれましたか。

88

練習問題

(1) **2**　***(2)*** **1**　***(3)*** **3**　***(4)*** **2**　***(5)*** **1**　***(6)*** **3**

解説

(1) **放送文** A: Mom, give me 20 dollars for my school trip.
B: When is the school trip?
A: Next Saturday, but I have to pay by tomorrow.
B: I see. Here you are.
Question: When does the boy have to pay for his school trip?

日本語訳 A：ママ，学校の遠足の費用20ドルちょうだい。
B：学校の遠足はいつなの？
A：来週の土曜日だけど，明日までに払わなければならないんだ。
B：わかったわ。はい，どうぞ。
質問：少年は学校の遠足の費用をいつ払わなければなりませんか。

▶ **1** 20ドル。　**2** 明日までに。
3 来週の土曜日。　**4** 学校の遠足のため。

(2) **放送文** A: Excuse me. Could you tell me how to get to the stadium?
B: Sure. Take the blue line and get off at the ‘City Museum Station.’
A: Is the stadium near that station?
B: Yes, about 5 minutes on foot.
Question: Where does the man want to go?

日本語訳 A：すみません。スタジアムへの行き方を教えていただけませんか。
B：はい。ブルー線に乗って，「市立博物館駅」で降りてください。
A：スタジアムはその駅から近いですか。
B：ええ，歩いて5分くらいです。
質問：男性はどこへ行きたいのですか。

▶ **1** スタジアム。　**2** 市立博物館。　**3** 駅。　**4** ブルー線。

(3) **放送文** A: Have you ever been to Tokyo?
B: Yes, twice. Last winter I went there.
A: I'll go there this summer for the first time. Can you tell me the spot you recommend?
B: Asakusa is a nice place. You can enjoy Japanese culture.
Question: How many times has the man been to Tokyo?

日本語訳 A: 東京には行ったことがありますか。
B: ええ，2回。この前の冬に，そこへ行きました。
A: この夏，私は初めてそこへ行く予定です。お勧めの場所はありますか。
B: 浅草はよい場所です。日本文化を楽しむことができます。
質問: 男性は何回東京に行ったことがありますか。

▶ **1** この前の夏。　**2** 浅草。　**3** 2回。　**4** 初めて。

(4) **放送文** A: Hello, welcome to Karaoke Studio. How many people?
B: Three. How much is the room fee?
A: Ten dollars per hour. How long would you like?
B: For two hours, please.
Question: How long will they sing *karaoke*?

日本語訳 A：こんにちは，カラオケスタジオへようこそ。何名様ですか。
B：3人です。部屋代はいくらですか。
A：1時間10ドルです。お時間はどうなさいますか。
B：2時間でお願いします。
質問：彼女らはカラオケをどれくらい歌う予定ですか。

▶ **1** 1時間。　**2** 2時間。　**3** 3時間。　**4** 4時間。

(5) **放送文** A: Hello, this is Kate speaking. Can I speak to William?
B: Sorry, Kate. He is out to get some books. Can I take a message?
A: Yes, please. Tomorrow, we need to take a camera for field work.
B: I'll tell him that.

Question: Why does Kate call William?

日本語訳　A：もしもし，ケイトです。ウィリアムはいますか。

B：ごめんなさい，ケイト。彼は本を買いに出かけているんです。伝言を承りましょうか。

A：お願いします。明日の実地調査に，カメラを持って行く必要があります。

B：彼にそれを伝えます。

質問：ケイトはなぜウィリアムに電話していますか。

▶ **1** カメラを持って行くことを伝えるため。

2 本を手に入れることを伝えるため。

3 伝言を受けることを伝えるため。

4 実地調査をすることを伝えるため。

(6) 放送文　A: Excuse me. How much is the T-shirt?

B: It's 20 dollars for one. If you buy two, they'll be 30 dollars.

A: Great! I'll take this blue one and that red one.

B: Thank you. I'll wrap them.

Question: How much is the T-shirt when we buy only one T-shirt?

日本語訳　A：すみません。そのTシャツはいくらですか。

B：1枚20ドルです。2枚お買い上げいただくと，（2枚で）30ドルです。

A：すごいわ。この青いのとあの赤いのをいただきます。

B：ありがとうございます。お包みいたします。

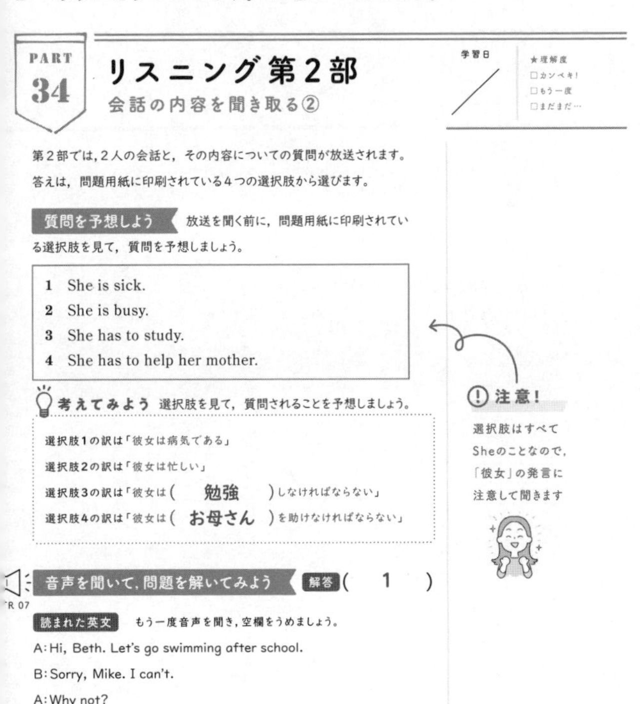
PART 34

リスニング第2部

会話の内容を聞き取る②

学習日 ／

★理解度
□カンペキ！
□もう一度
□まだまだ…

第2部では，2人の会話と，その内容についての質問が放送されます。
答えは，問題用紙に印刷されている4つの選択肢から選びます。

質問を予想しよう　放送を聞く前に，問題用紙に印刷されている選択肢を見て，質問を予想しましょう。

1 She is sick.
2 She is busy.
3 She has to study.
4 She has to help her mother.

考えてみよう　選択肢を見て，質問されることを予想しましょう。

選択肢1の訳は「彼女は病気である」
選択肢2の訳は「彼女は忙しい」
選択肢3の訳は「彼女は（　勉強　）しなければならない」
選択肢4の訳は「彼女は（　お母さん　）を助けなければならない」

注意！
選択肢はすべてSheのことなので，「彼女」の発言に注意して聞きます

TR 07

音声を聞いて，問題を解いてみよう　解答（　1　）

読まれた英文　もう一度音声を聞き，空欄をうめましょう。

A: Hi, Beth. Let's go swimming after school.
B: Sorry, Mike. I can't.
A: Why not?
B: I have a (cold), so I want to go home early today.
QUESTION: (Why) won't Beth go swimming with Mike today?

日本語訳
A: やあ，ベス。放課後泳ぎに行こうよ。
B: ごめんね，マイク。行けないの。
A: どうして？
B: 風邪をひいたから，今日は早く家に帰りたいの。
質問：ベスはなぜ今日マイクと泳ぎに行かないのですか。

90

質問：Tシャツを1枚だけ買うといくらですか。

▶ **1** 10ドル。 **2** 15ドル。 **3** 20ドル。 **4** 30ドル。

練習問題

***(1)* 3　*(2)* 4　*(3)* 2　*(4)* 3　*(5)* 1　*(6)* 4**

解説

(1) 放送文　A: Hi, Nozomi. I visited Japan with my family during summer vacation.

B: Hi, Liam. Really? What city did you visit?

A: Tokyo. I wanted to visit Kyoto and Osaka, but I couldn't.

B: You can go there next time. Then I will guide you.

Question: Which city did Liam visit in Japan?

日本語訳　A：こんにちは，ノゾミ。僕は夏休みに家族と日本を訪れたんだ。

B：こんにちは，リアム。本当？　どの都市を訪れたの？

A：東京だよ。京都と大阪も行きたかったけど，行けなかったんだ。

B：次回行けるわよ。そのときは私が案内するわ。

質問：リアムは日本のどの都市を訪れましたか。

▶ **1** 京都。 **2** 大阪。 **3** 東京。 **4** 札幌。

(2) 放送文　A: May I have your order?

B: I'll have a steak and rice, please.

A: Would you like something to drink?

B: Coffee, please.

Question: What did the man order?

日本語訳 A：ご注文は何になさいますか。
B：ステーキとライスをください。
A：何かお飲み物はいかがですか。
B：コーヒーをください。
質問：男性は何を頼みましたか。

▶ **1** ステーキとライス。
2 ステーキとコーヒー。
3 ステーキとパンとコーヒー。
4 ステーキとライスとコーヒー。

(3) 放送文 A: Jill, do you have time to talk about next week's class party?
B: Sorry, I'm busy now. How about after class?
A: I have to go home early today. Will you give me a call tonight, then?
B: OK. I'll call you around eight.
Question: When will they talk about the party?

日本語訳 A：ジル，来週のクラスのパーティーについて話す時間はあるかい？
B：ごめんなさい，今忙しいの。授業のあとはどう？
A：今日は早く帰らなければならないんだ。そしたら，夜，僕に電話をくれるかい？
B：わかったわ。8時頃に電話するわね。
質問：彼らはいつパーティーについて話しますか。

▶ **1** 今日の授業のあと。 **2** 今夜。 **3** 明日。 **4** 来週。

(4) 放送文 A: Hi, Christy. Let's go to the beach after school.
B: Hi, John. It will rain this afternoon. The TV said so this morning.
A: Oh, too bad. Then how about seeing a movie?
B: OK. I bought a new DVD yesterday. Please come to my house.
Question: What will they do this afternoon?

日本語訳 A：やあ，クリスティ。放課後，ビーチに行こうよ。
B：こんにちは，ジョン。今日の午後は雨が降るわよ。テレビ番組で今朝そう言っていたわ。
A：ああ，残念だ。それなら映画を見るのはどう？
B：いいわよ。昨日，新しいDVDを買ったのよ。私の家に来て。
質問：今日の午後に，彼らは何をするつもりですか。

▶ **1** 映画館に行く。 **2** ビーチに行く。
3 クリスティの家に行く。 **4** ジョンの家に行く。

(5) 放送文 A: Dad, I have to go to Peterson College next Sunday. How can I get there?
B: Well, Jenifer. You can go there by train or bus.
A: Which is faster? I have to get there by eight.
B: I see. Then, I'll drive you to the college.
Question: How will Jenifer go to Peterson College?

日本語訳 A：パパ，来週の日曜にピーターソン大学に行かなければならないの。そこへはどうやって行くの？
B：そうだね，ジェニファー。そこへは電車かバスで行くことができるよ。
A：どっちが早いの？ 8時までにそこに着かなければならないのよ。
B：わかったよ。じゃあ，僕が大学まで車で送ってあげるよ。
質問：ジェニファーはどうやってピーターソン大学に行く予定ですか。

▶ **1** 車で。 **2** 電車で。 **3** バスで。 **4** 徒歩で。

(6) 放送文 A: Ashley, is this your bag?
B: No, I think it's Nicole's, David.
A: I see. Do you know where Bob's bag is?
B: It's that blue one on the desk.
Question: Whose bag is it on the desk?

日本語訳 A：アシュリー，これは君のかばんかい？
B：いいえ，それはニコルのだと思うわ，デビッド。
A：わかったよ。ボブのかばんがどこにあるか知ってる？
B：机の上の青いのよ。
質問：机の上にはだれのかばんがありますか。

▶ **1** デビッドのかばん。 **2** アシュリーのかばん。
3 ニコルのかばん。 **4** ボブのかばん。

PART 35

リスニング第3部

英文の内容を聞き取る①

学習日 ／

★理解度
□カンペキ!
□もう一度
□まだまだ…

リスニング第3部は，短い英文が放送されます。その後，英文の内容に関する質問が放送されるので，その答えを問題用紙に印刷されている選択肢の中から選びます。

質問を予想しよう 放送を聞く前に，問題用紙に印刷されている選択肢を見て，質問を予想しましょう。

1	Tennis.	2	Soccer.
3	Swimming.	4	Golf.

①注意！
選択肢はすべて「スポーツ」だとわかります

考えてみよう 選択肢を見て，質問されることを予想しましょう。

選択肢1の訳は「テニス」　選択肢2の訳は「サッカー」
選択肢3の訳は「（ 水泳 ）」　選択肢4の訳は「（ ゴルフ ）」

音声を聞いて，問題を解いてみよう 解答（ 2 ）

読まれた英文 もう一度音声を聞き，空欄をうめましょう。

Steve likes sports. He plays tennis and golf with his family. He has a swimming lesson on weekends. But his (favorite) sport is soccer. He always enjoys watching it on TV.
QUESTION: (Which) sport does Steve like best?

日本語訳

スティーブはスポーツが好きです。彼は家族と一緒にテニスとゴルフをします。週末に水泳を習っています。でも，彼のお気に入りのスポーツはサッカーです。いつもテレビで見て楽しんでいます。
質問：スティーブはどのスポーツがいちばん好きですか。

練習問題

(1) 3　(2) 3　(3) 3　(4) 2　(5) 1　(6) 4

解説

(1) **放送文** Welcome, everyone. Cynthia Evan's piano concert will start in ten minutes. Please turn off your cellphones now. Also, you can't take any photos during the concert. We hope you'll enjoy her performance.
Question: What should people do now?
日本語訳 皆さま，ご来場ありがとうございます。シンシア・エバンによるピアノコンサートは10分以内に開始予定です。今のうちに携帯電話の電源を切ってください。また，コンサートの間はいかなる写真撮影もご遠慮ください。彼女の演奏を楽しんでいただけたら幸いです。
質問：人々は今何をすべきですか。
▶ 1 写真を撮る。　2 バイオリンを弾く。
3 携帯電話の電源を切る。　4 食べ物と飲み物を買う。

(2) **放送文** Allan and his family have a plan to climb a mountain tomorrow, but it has been raining for three days. They are now thinking they will not go to the mountain and will have a party at home instead.
Question: What will they do tomorrow?
日本語訳 アランと彼の家族には，明日登山する計画がありますが，3日間ずっと雨が降っています。彼らは今，山には行かず，代わりに家でパーティーをしようかと考えています。
質問：彼らは明日何をする予定ですか。
▶ 1 山に登る。　2 ハイキングに行く。
3 家でパーティーをする。　4 映画を見る。

(3) **放送文** Erika studied English hard for three years, and passed the foreign exchange exam. She will study in California for a year. To brush up her English, she's going to have English lessons three times per week until she leaves.
Question: How long will Erika study in California?
日本語訳 エリカは3年間一生懸命英語を勉強し，交換留学の試験に合格しました。彼女は1年間カリフォルニアで勉強する予定です。彼女は自分の英語を磨くために，出発までに週に3回英語のレッスンを受けるつもりです。
質問：エリカはどのくらい長くカリフォルニアで勉強する予定ですか。
▶ 1 1週間。　2 3週間。　3 1年間。　4 3年間。

(4) **放送文** Yesterday, I lost my watch. I looked around for it, but I couldn't find it. I really felt down because it was my favorite one my father gave me. However, my mother found it under the sofa this morning. I was very glad, thanks to Mom.
Question: What happened yesterday?
日本語訳 昨日，私は腕時計をなくしました。私はそれをあちこち探しましたが，見つけられませんでした。その時計は父が私にくれたお気に入りのものだったので，とても落ち込みました。しかし，母が今朝ソファの下でそれを見つけてくれました。私はとてもうれしくて母に感謝しています。
質問：昨日，何がありましたか。
▶ 1 時計をあげた。　2 時計をなくした。
3 時計を見た。　4 時計を見つけた。

(5) **放送文** Attention, students. Tomorrow we will join the city chorus contest. We'll meet at 9 o'clock in front of the City Hall. We'll practice once at the Hall, and have lunch. Don't forget to take your lunch. The contest will start at one.
Question: What will the students do tomorrow morning?
日本語訳 生徒の皆さん，注目してください。明日，私たちは市の合唱コンテストに参加します。市のホールの前に9時に集合です。私たちはホールで一度練習し，昼食をとります。自分の昼食を持ってくるのを忘れないでください。コンテストは1時に始まります。

質問：生徒たちは明日の朝，何をするつもりですか。

▶ **1** 合唱の練習をする。 **2** 学校で会う。
3 昼食をとる。 **4** コンテストに参加する。

(6) 放送文 Austyn bought a new smartphone last week. He was happy to get it because it has a high-performance camera with three lenses. He went on a short trip to take pictures this weekend.
Question: What did Austyn go on a short trip for?

日本語訳 オースティンは先週新しいスマートフォンを買いました。それは，3つのレンズがついた高機能カメラがついているので，それを手に入れて彼はうれしく思いました。彼は今週末，写真を撮るために小旅行に行きました。
質問：オースティンは何をしに小旅行に行きましたか。

▶ **1** 3つのカメラレンズを手に入れる。
2 新しいスマートフォンを買う。
3 小旅行に行く。
4 写真を撮る。

PART 36

リスニング第3部

英文の内容を聞き取る②

学習日

★理解度
□カンペキ！
□もう一度
□まだまだ…

リスニング第3部は，短い英文が放送されます。その後，英文の内容に関する質問が放送されるので，その答えを問題用紙に印刷されている選択肢の中から選びます。

質問を予想しよう 放送を聞く前に，問題用紙に印刷されている選択肢を見て，質問を予想しましょう。

1 Buy some salad.	**2** Make breakfast.
3 Teach French to her.	**4** Help her in the office.

考えてみよう 選択肢を見て，質問されることを予想しましょう。

選択肢1の訳は「サラダを買う」
選択肢2の訳は「朝食を作る」
選択肢3の訳は「（ フランス語 ）を彼女に教える」
選択肢4の訳は「（ オフィス ）で彼女を手伝う」

注意！
選択肢はすべて「行動，動作」なので，「だれが何をするか」に注意して聞きます

TR 11

音声を聞いて，問題を解いてみよう 解答（ 2 ）

読まれた英文 もう一度音声を聞き，空欄をうめましょう。

I have to go to work earlier tomorrow. I won't have time to (cook) breakfast, so I asked my daughter to do it. She's going to prepare French toast and salad. She's really helpful.
QUESTION: (What) did the woman (ask) her daughter to do?

日本語訳
私は明日早く仕事に行かなければなりません。朝食を作る時間がないので，娘に頼みました。彼女はフレンチトーストとサラダを準備するつもりです。彼女は本当に助けになります。
質問：女性は娘に何をするように頼みましたか。

94

練習問題

(1) **4** ***(2)*** **1** ***(3)*** **3** ***(4)*** **1** ***(5)*** **4** ***(6)*** **2**

解説

(1) 放送文 I visit Canada with my family every year. We usually go there in spring or fall, but my favorite time to go is around New Year's Day. I enjoy sports such as skiing and skating. I've never been there in summer.
Question: Which is the boy's favorite season to visit Canada?

日本語訳 僕は毎年家族とカナダを訪れます。僕たちはたいてい春か秋にそこへ行きますが，僕が行くのが好きな時期は元日のあたりです。僕は例えばスキーやスケートなどのスポーツを楽しみます。僕は夏にそこに行ったことはありません。
質問：少年がカナダを訪れるのにお気に入りの季節はどれですか。

▶ **1** 春。 **2** 夏。 **3** 秋。 **4** 冬。

(2) 放送文 Welcome to the Westwood Express Bus ticket office. The bus for London leaves every 30 minutes. The next one will leave at one o'clock. Don't forget to buy your tickets at least

15 minutes before that.
Question: What time will the next express bus leave?
日本語訳 ウェストウッド急行バスチケット売り場へようこそ。ロンドン行きのバスは30分ごとに出ています。次のバスは1時に出発します。少なくとも出発15分前までにチケットを買うのを忘れないようにしてください。
質問：次の急行バスは何時に出ますか。
▶ **1** 1時。 **2** 1時15分。 **3** 1時30分。 **4** 1時45分。

(3) 放送文 I have a best friend, his name is Daniel. Since he lives next to my house, we always go to school together, and play soccer, baseball, and so on. Next month, he and his family will move to Australia. I will really miss him very much.
Question: What is the boy talking about?
日本語訳 僕には親友がいて，名前はダニエルです。彼は僕の家の隣に住んでいるので，僕たちはいつも一緒に学校へ行き，サッカーや野球などをします。来月，彼と彼の家族はオーストラリアに引っ越す予定です。僕は彼がいなくなって，本当に寂しく思うでしょう。
質問：少年は何について話していますか。
▶ **1** 学校への行き方。
2 サッカーや野球などのスポーツ。
3 彼の隣に住んでいる友人。
4 来月オーストラリアに行くこと。

(4) 放送文 I usually have piano lessons on Tuesdays and Fridays. However, my teacher is going on a trip, and Tuesday's lesson has been moved to Wednesday this week. Now I have one day to practice the piano for Wednesday's lesson.
Question: What day of the week is it today?
日本語訳 私はふだん火曜日と金曜日にピアノのレッスンを受けています。しかし先生が旅行に行くため，今週の火曜日のレッスンは水曜日に変更になりました。よって今は，私は水曜日のレッスンのためにピアノを練習する日が1日あります。
質問：今日は何曜日ですか。
▶ **1** 火曜日。 **2** 水曜日。 **3** 木曜日。 **4** 金曜日。

(5) 放送文 Thank you for shopping at Jones Supermarket. There will be a special sale at the meat corner in ten minutes. All meat will be 30 percent off for only one hour. Come to the meat corner and save money!
Question: How long will the meat be on sale?
日本語訳 ジョーンズスーパーマーケットでのお買い物をありがとうございます。10分以内にお肉売り場にて，特別セールをいたします。すべてのお肉が1時間だけ30パーセント引きになります。ぜひお肉売り場に来ていただき，節約してください！
質問：どれくらい長くお肉はセールになりますか。
▶ **1** 10分。 **2** 30分。 **3** 45分。 **4** 1時間。

(6) 放送文 Dylan wanted to give a necklace to his girlfriend, but he didn't have enough money to buy it. His sister Emily knew that, and asked him to take care of her children as a part time job. He'll buy the necklace in one more week.
Question: What is Dylan doing to buy a present for his girlfriend?
日本語訳 ディランはガールフレンドにネックレスをあげたかったのですが，それを買うための十分なお金を持っていませんでした。彼の姉のエミリーはそれを知って，彼に自分の子どもの世話をするアルバイトを頼みました。彼はもう1週間すればネックレスを買うでしょう。
質問：ディランはガールフレンドにプレゼントを買うために何をしていますか。
▶ **1** ネックレスを売っている。
2 アルバイトをしている。
3 彼の姉の世話をしている。
4 彼のガールフレンドを手伝っている。

模擬試験　解答一覧

注意事項

①解答にはHBの黒鉛筆（シャープペンシルも可）を使用し，解答を訂正する場合には消しゴムで完全に消してください。

②解答用紙は絶対に汚したり折り曲げたり，所定以外のところへの記入はしないでください。

③マーク例

良い例	悪い例

これ以下の濃さのマークは読めません。

解答欄

問題番号		1 2 3 4
1	(1)	① ❷ ③ ④
	(2)	① ② ❸ ④
	(3)	① ② ❸ ④
	(4)	❶ ② ③ ④
	(5)	① ② ③ ❹
	(6)	① ❷ ③ ④
	(7)	❶ ② ③ ④
	(8)	① ❷ ③ ④
	(9)	① ② ③ ❹
	(10)	① ❷ ③ ④
	(11)	① ② ❸ ④
	(12)	❶ ② ③ ④
	(13)	① ② ❸ ④
	(14)	① ② ③ ❹
	(15)	❶ ② ③ ④

解答欄

問題番号		1 2 3 4
2	(16)	① ② ③ ❹
	(17)	❶ ② ③ ④
	(18)	① ❷ ③ ④
	(19)	❶ ② ③ ④
	(20)	❶ ② ③ ④
3	(21)	① ❷ ③ ④
	(22)	① ② ❸ ④
	(23)	① ② ❸ ④
	(24)	① ② ❸ ④
	(25)	① ② ③ ❹
	(26)	❶ ② ③ ④
	(27)	① ② ❸ ④
	(28)	① ② ③ ❹
	(29)	① ❷ ③ ④
	(30)	① ② ③ ❹

リスニング解答欄

問題番号		1 2 3 4
第1部	No.1	❶ ② ③
	No.2	① ❷ ③
	No.3	① ② ❸
	No.4	❶ ② ③
	No.5	① ❷ ③
	No.6	① ② ❸
	No.7	❶ ② ③
	No.8	❶ ② ③
	No.9	① ② ❸
	No.10	❶ ② ③

リスニング解答欄

問題番号		1 2 3 4
第2部	No.11	① ② ❸ ④
	No.12	① ② ③ ❹
	No.13	❶ ② ③ ④
	No.14	① ② ❸ ④
	No.15	① ❷ ③ ④
	No.16	① ② ❸ ④
	No.17	① ② ❸ ④
	No.18	① ② ③ ❹
	No.19	① ② ③ ❹
	No.20	① ❷ ③ ④

リスニング解答欄

問題番号		1 2 3 4
第3部	No.21	❶ ② ③ ④
	No.22	❶ ② ③ ④
	No.23	① ❷ ③ ④
	No.24	① ② ❸ ④
	No.25	① ② ❸ ④
	No.26	① ② ❸ ④
	No.27	① ② ❸ ④
	No.28	① ❷ ③ ④
	No.29	① ② ❸ ④
	No.30	① ② ③ ❹

※④⑤の解答例はP37にあります。

筆記

1

(1) 2	**(2) 3**	**(3) 3**	**(4) 1**	**(5) 4**
(6) 2	**(7) 1**	**(8) 2**	**(9) 4**	**(10) 2**
(11) 3	**(12) 1**	**(13) 3**	**(14) 4**	**(15) 1**

(1) 正解 **2**
この2つのかばんは同じように見えます。それらの違いは何ですか。
▶ **1** 選手権　**2** 違い　**3** 行動　**4** 約束

(2) 正解 **3**
走る必要はないよ，スティーブ。次のバスに間に合うには十分な時間があるよ。
▶ **1** 素早い　**2** 暑い　**3** 十分な　**4** 晴れた

(3) 正解 **3**
A：ヘンリー，テーブルの上のはさみを取ってくれる？　この箱を開けるのに必要なんだ。
B：いいよ。はい，どうぞ。
▶ **1** ホチキス　**2** 店　**3** はさみ　**4** くつ

(4) 正解 **1**
A：すみません。娘用のおもちゃを探しているのですが。
B：4階でお求めいただけますよ。
▶ **1** 階　**2** 授業　**3** 紹介　**4** 予定

(5) 正解 **4**
A：フレッド，何を読んでいるの？
B：僕の大好きな作家の新しい小説だよ。昨日，買ったんだ。
▶ **1** 自転車　**2** スーツケース
3 言語　**4** 小説

(6) 正解 **2**
A：テッドは入院しているの？　何があったの？
B：今朝，車にはねられたんだよ。
▶ **1** 変わった　**2** 起きた
3 説明した　**4** 焼いた

(7) 正解 **1**
イタリアンレストランはあそこだね。道を渡らないといけないよ。
▶ **1** ～を渡る　**2** ～をつかまえる
3 ～をえがく　**4** ～を救う

(8) 正解 **2**
A：すみません。郵便局はどこでしょうか。
B：ここから近いですよ。まっすぐ行って，あの角を右に曲がってください。
▶ **1** 注文する　**2** 曲がる
3 支払う　**4** 決める

(9) 正解 **4**
昨夜は遅くまで勉強しました。今，試験の準備はできています。
▶ **1** まちがった　**2** おいしい
3 ひとりで　**4** 準備ができて

(10) 正解 **2**
A：君のお姉さんは野球に興味があるの？
B：うん。彼女はしょっちゅう球場に行っているわよ。
▶ **1** 心配な　**2** 興味を持った
3 打たれた　**4** 開催された

(11) 正解 **3**
A：今日，さくらんぼパイを焼いたの。食べてみたい？
B：ありがとう，モニカ。一切れもらえるといいな。
▶ **1** 一覧　**2** テーブル　**3** 一切れ　**4** クラブ

(12) 正解 **1**
A：次の電車はどのくらい待つ必要がありますか。
B：ああ，ほんの数分ですよ。
▶ **1** 2つ　**2** びん
3 カウンター　**4** 接触

(13) 正解 **3**
私のいとこはマックスという小さな黒い犬を飼っています。
解説 〈名詞＋過去分詞＋語句〉の形で，後ろから名詞を説明しています。

(14) 正解 **4**
マリアにとって，日本語を話すのは簡単ではありません。
解説 〈It is[It's] ～ for 人 to ....〉「(人) にとって…することは～です」

(15) 正解 **1**
A：ジムと話している女性を知っている？
B：彼のお姉さんのケイトだよ。
解説 (　　) の前が「人」なので，whoを入れます。

2

(16) 4 (17) 1 (18) 2 (19) 1 (20) 1

(16) 正解 **4**

母親：あなたの妹はどうして泣いているの？
息子：家に帰る途中に走っていて，転んだんだよ。

▶ **1** 今日は晴れているよ。
2 それは彼女のかばんだよ。
3 彼女は喜ぶだろうね。

(17) 正解 **1**

孫娘：おばあちゃん，クッキーを食べてもいい？
祖母：もちろんよ，サリー。遠慮なくどうぞ。

▶ **2** その通りよ。　**3** 全力を尽くしてね。
4 そう思わないわね。

(18) 正解 **2**

男の子：水曜までに歴史のレポートを終わらせなくちゃいけないよ。君のはもう終わった？
女の子：ちょうど提出したところよ。週末のほとんどをそれに費やしたわ。

▶ **1** 歴史は好き？　**3** 君の歴史の先生はだれ？
4 フィラデルフィアに行ったことはある？

(19) 正解 **1**

男性：どのくらいの頻度で札幌を訪れますか。
女性：私はそこへ，年に2回行きます。

▶ **2** 5日間　**3** シーフードを楽しむために
4 そして今回は旭川にも

(20) 正解 **1**

客：コーヒーをもう一杯いただけますか。
ウェイター：かしこまりました。すぐにお持ちします。

▶ **2** いらっしゃいませ。　**3** あまりよくありません。
4 こちらがメニューです。

3[A]

(21) 2 (22) 3

ハミルトン美術館だより

・特別展
19～20世紀のカナダ人芸術家による絵画の特別展が始まりました!
入館料：
大人：2ドル
学生：1ドル
シニア（60歳以上）：無料
子ども（18歳以下）：無料

・案内付きツアー
当館の美術ガイドの1人が同行する無料の案内付きツアーにご参加ください！　ミニツアーは30分間で，平日は午後2時30分に，週末は午前11時に開始します。ハイライトツアーは1時間で，週末の午後1時に開始します。ツアーは2階の北入り口から始めます。

当館は午前10時から午後6時まで，
毎日開館しています。

詳細は，当館のウェブサイトまで：
http://www.hamiltonartmuseum.com

(21) 正解 **2**

もしあなたが～なら，あなたは特別展を見るのに2ドル支払います。

▶ **1** 70歳　**2** 50歳
3 学生　**4** 美術館ガイド

(22) 正解 **3**

ハイライトツアーは何時に始まりますか。

▶ **1** 午前10時に。　**2** 午前11時に。
3 午後1時に。　**4** 午後2時30分に。

3[B]

(23) 3	(24) 3	(25) 4

送信者：フジモト・マミ
受信者：イライザ・ウィリアムズ
日付：11月27日
件名：シドニーを訪れる予定です!

こんにちは，イライザ!
あなたとご主人はいかがお過ごしですか。私がシドニーを去ってからもう5年が過ぎました。私はいつも戻りたいと思っていました。そしてついに，またあなた方を訪ねることができます！　ご存じのように，私はオーストラリアにいくつかオフィスを持つ日本の会社で働いていますが，そのうちの2か所を訪れる予定なのです。まずメルボルンに，12月14日に到着します。その翌日は会議があります。16日に，シドニーへ移動します。17日に別の会議があり，その夜，日本へ戻る飛行機に乗らなければなりません。16日にお時間はありますか。そのときにあなた方を訪ねたいと思っています。
お返事お待ちしています。
マミ

送信者：イライザ・ウィリアムズ
受信者：フジモト・マミ
日付：11月28日
件名：おかえりなさい!

こんにちは，マミ!
メールをどうもありがとう。ええ，16日は空いているわ。夫のジョージが昨年，仕事をやめたので，私たちは以前よりもっと時間があるの。現在，わが家にはハルという日本出身の別の学生がいます。彼女は大学で経営を学んでいるのよ。5年前のあなたと全く同じね。彼女は来年の1月までここにいるので，あなたも彼女に会えるわ。彼女は日本での就職についてあなたに尋ねたいと言っているの，だからあなたの経験を彼女に話してあげてください。あなたはメルボルンから飛行機で来る予定ですか。私たちは空港に車で迎えに行きます。到着時間を教えてください。
ではまたね。
イライザ

(23) 正解 **3**

マミは，～シドニーへ来ます。

- **1** 観光のために　**2** 経営を勉強するために
- **3** 仕事で　**4** 姉［妹］に会うために

(24) 正解 **3**

マミはいつシドニーを発ちますか。

- **1** 12月15日に。　**2** 12月16日に。
- **3** 12月17日に。　**4** 12月18日に。

(25) 正解 **4**

ハルはシドニーで何をしていますか。

- **1** 日本の会社で働いている。
- **2** 日本語を教えている。
- **3** 住む家を探している。
- **4** 大学で勉強している。

3[C]

(26) 1	(27) 3	(28) 4	(29) 2	(30) 4

ドリームキャッチャー

アメリカやカナダに行くと，どこかでドリームキャッチャーを見つけるかもしれません。それは，クモの巣のような網のついた輪で，網の中央には穴が開いています。眺めて楽しむために，自分の部屋の壁にドリームキャッチャーをかける人が多いですが，それらはどこから来たのでしょうか。

ドリームキャッチャーの起源はオジブワ族の文化にあります。オジブワ族とはアメリカとカナダに住む部族の１つです。1800年代中ごろ，ドリームキャッチャーは悪い夢から子どもを守るために使われると，ヨーロッパから来た人々は書き記しました。

クモの巣が虫を捕まえるように，ドリームキャッチャーは悪い夢を捕まえると，オジブワ族の人々は信じています。朝になると，日光がドリームキャッチャーに当たって，捕まえた悪い夢を焼き払うのです。ところが，よい夢は網を通りぬけて，眠っている子どもにたどり着くことができます。このようにして，子どもたちは夜によい夢だけを見ることができるのです。

今日，ドリームキャッチャーはより色鮮やかなものになっています。それらはさまざまな素材で装飾されています。このようなドリームキャッチャーはとても美しいので，アメリカやカナダのおみやげとして人気があります。一方，素朴なドリームキャッチャーを作るのは難しくないので，子どもたちはしばしば，学校で自分自身のドリームキャッチャーを作り，教室の壁にかけます。

(26) 正解 1

多くの人々はどのようにしてドリームキャッチャーを使いますか。

▶ 1 部屋の中で見て楽しむ。
2 アメリカやカナダに持っていく。
3 網の中央の穴を閉じる。
4 クモを捕まえて中に入れておく。

(27) 正解 3

だれが初めてドリームキャッチャーを作りましたか。

▶ 1 カナダに移住した人々。
2 ヨーロッパに移住したカナダ人。
3 北アメリカのオジブワ族の人々。
4 子どもを持つアメリカ人。

(28) 正解 4

1800年代中ごろ，ヨーロッパから来た人々は，～と書き記しました。

▶ 1 オジブワ族の人々はドリームキャッチャーを売ってお金を手に入れた。
2 オジブワ族の子どもたちはドリームキャッチャーを怖がった。
3 オジブワ族の人々からドリームキャッチャーの作り方を教わった。
4 ドリームキャッチャーの目的は，子どもたちを守ることであった。

(29) 正解 2

ドリームキャッチャーはどのように役立ちますか。

▶ 1 よい夢を作り出す。
2 悪い夢を取りのぞく。
3 何か運のよいものをもたらす。
4 よいアイディアを与える。

(30) 正解 4

これは何についての話ですか。

▶ 1 子どもたちに夢を与える特別な行事。
2 世界で最も有名なお土産の1つ。
3 子どもたちをクモや昆虫から守る方法の1つ。
4 今日も人気のある伝統的製品。

4

Hi,

Your little sister is so cute! I saw her at the supermarket with your mother today. How old is she? Do you have any other brothers or sisters? I wish I had a little sister, too.

Your friend,
Jane

Eメール訳

こんにちは，

あなたの妹はとてもかわいいですね！　今日，スーパーマーケットであなたのお母さんと一緒にいるところを見ました。彼女は何歳ですか。ほかにも兄弟や姉妹がいますか。私にも妹がいたらいいのにと思います。

あなたの友達，

ジェーン

Hi, Jane!
こんにちは，ジェーン！
Thank you for your e-mail.
Eメールをありがとう。

解答例1

I didn't know you saw them. My sister is five. I don't have any other brothers or sisters. However, I wish I had a brother. （25語）

解答例2

I think she's cute, too! She is only two years old. I also have three older brothers. There are many people in our house. （24語）

Best wishes,
幸せを願って

解答例1訳

あなたが彼女たちを見たのは知りませんでした。私の妹は5歳です。私にはほかの兄弟や姉妹はいません。でも，兄弟が1人いたらいいのにと思います。

解答例2訳

私も彼女はかわいいと思います！　彼女はたったの2歳です。私には兄も3人います。私たちの家にはたくさんの人がいます。

5

質問

あなたは春と夏の，どちらが好きですか。

解答例1

I like spring better. I have two reasons. First, it's not too hot like summer, so I can spend a long time outside. Second, I can enjoy watching beautiful cherry blossoms (during this season). （31-34語）

解答例1訳

私は春のほうが好きです。それには2つの理由があります。第一に，夏のように暑すぎないので，屋外で長い時間を過ごすことができます。第二に，（この季節の間は）美しい桜の花を見るのを楽しむことができます。

解答例2

I like summer better. First, I have (a) long vacation, so I can spend much time for my hobby. Second, I have hay fever, so I often have a bad headache in spring. （32-33語）

解答例2訳

私は夏のほうが好きです。第一に，長い休みがあるので，多くの時間を自分の趣味のために使うことができます。第二に，私は花粉症なので，春にはしばしばひどい頭痛があります。

リスニング

第1部

No. 1 1	*No. 2* 2	*No. 3* 3	*No. 4* 1
No. 5 2	*No. 6* 3	*No. 7* 1	*No. 8* 1
No. 9 3	*No. 10* 1		

No. 1 正解 **1**

A: This chocolate cake looks delicious.

B: Yes. But that apple pie looks good, too.

A: Which one shall we get?

▶ *1* Can we have both?

2 You are right.

3 I like your shirt.

訳 A：このチョコレートケーキはとてもおいしそうに見えるよ。

B：ええ。でも，あのアップルパイもおいしそう。

A：どれを買おうか？

▶ *1* 両方買ってもいい？

2 そのとおりだね。

3 あなたのシャツ，いいわね。

No. 2 正解 **2**

A: You look tired.

B: Last night, I did my homework until midnight.

A: Well, don't stay up late tonight.

▶ *1* Yes, please.

2 I won't.

3 I'll call you.

訳 A：疲れているみたいだね。

B：昨夜，真夜中まで宿題をしたのよ。

A：じゃあ，今夜は遅くまで起きてちゃだめだよ。

▶ *1* ええ，お願いね。

2 しないわ。

3 電話するね。

No. 3 正解 **3**

A: Hello. Is Mr. Parker there?

B: I'm afraid he's in a meeting now.

A: When will he be back?

▶ *1* On the third floor.

2 On the phone.

3 In thirty minutes.

訳 A：こんにちは。そちらにパーカーさんはいらっしゃいますか。

B：あいにくただいま会議中です。

A：いつ戻られますか。

▶ *1* 3階に。

2 電話中です。

3 30分以内には。

No. 4 正解 **1**

A: I didn't see you in the afternoon yesterday.

B: I had a headache, so I went home.

A: I hope you're feeling better today.

▶ *1* I am, thank you.

2 To the doctor.

3 I can help you.

訳 A：昨日の午後，君を見かけなかったよ。

B：頭痛がしたので帰宅したの。

A：今日は具合がよくなっているといいんだけど。

▶ *1* なっているわ，ありがとう。

2 医者へ。

3 あなたを手伝えるわよ。

No. 5 正解 **2**

A: Excuse me.

B: Yes, Pamela?

A: I left my textbook in the locker.

▶ *1* I'll give you this pencil.

2 Hurry up and get it.

3 I had breakfast.

訳 A：すみません。

B：何ですか，パルマ。

A：ロッカーに教科書を置いてきてしまいました。

▶ *1* この鉛筆をあげよう。

2 急いで取ってきなさい。

3 私は朝食を食べました。

No. 6 正解 **3**

A: Are you enjoying the game, Monica?

B: Yes, Bill. It's exciting.

A: Have you watched basketball before?

▶ *1* It's cold today.

2 I like playing the guitar.

3 This is the first time.

訳 A：モニカ，試合を楽しんでる？

B：ええ，ビル。わくわくするわね。

A：以前にバスケットボールを見たことはあるの？

▶ *1* 今日は寒いわね。

2 ギターを弾くのが好きよ。

3 これが初めてよ。

No. 7 正解 **1**

A: What are you doing, Mike?

B: Watching videos. These cats are so cute.

A: Can I have a look?

▶ *1* Sure. Come here.

2 Yes. I'm hungry.

3 I prefer dogs.

訳 A：マイク，何をしているの？

B：動画を見ているんだよ。この猫たちがとてもかわいいんだ。

A：ちょっと見せてくれる？

▶ *1* いいよ。こっちに来て。

2 うん。おなかがすいているんだ。

3 犬のほうが好きだよ。

No. 8 正解 **1**

A: What are you reading, Terry?

B: I'm just looking at this Korean book.

A: Do you study Korean?

▶ *1* I'm going to.

2 Well, I can't speak Chinese.

3 I like cooking.

訳 A：テリー，何を読んでいるの？

B：この韓国語の本をちょっと見ているんだ。

A：韓国語を勉強しているの？

▶ *1* その予定なんだよ。

2 えっと，中国語は話せないよ。

3 料理をするのが好きだよ。

No. 9 正解 **3**

A: Don't forget your umbrella, Beth.

B: Why? It's sunny today.

A: It's going to rain this afternoon.

▶ *1* Around six.

2 I've been there twice.

3 All right. I'll take it.

訳 A：傘を忘れないで，ベス。

B：どうして？ 今日は晴れているわ。

A：今日の午後は雨が降りそうだよ。

▶ *1* 6時ごろに。

2 そこへは二度行ったことがあるわ。

3 わかった。持っていくね。

No. 10 正解 **1**

A: What did you do last weekend?

B: I went to Lake Louise.

A: Oh, that area is really beautiful.

▶ *1* Yes. It's my favorite place.

2 I didn't go there.

3 We have to finish it.

訳 A：先週末は何をしたの？

B：ルイーズ湖に行ったよ。

A：ああ，あの場所は本当にきれいよね。

▶ *1* うん。僕の大好きな場所なんだ。

2 そこへは行かなかったよ。

3 僕たちはそれを終わらせなきゃいけないよ。

第2部

No. 11 3	No. 12 4	No. 13 1	No. 14 3
No. 15 2	No. 16 3	No. 17 3	No. 18 4
No. 19 4	No. 20 2		

No. 11 正解 3

A: Let's go to the Italian restaurant for lunch today.
B: Oh, I had dinner there last night. How about the Korean restaurant?
A: I think it's closed today. Shall we try that new Japanese restaurant?
B: OK.
Question: What kind of food will they eat for lunch today?

訳 A：今日，昼食はイタリアンレストランに行こうよ。
B：ああ，昨夜そこで夕食を食べたのよ。韓国料理店はどう？
A：そこは今日は閉まっていると思うよ。あの新しい日本料理店を試してみようか？
B：いいわよ。
質問：彼らは今日，昼食に何料理を食べますか。
▶ *1* 韓国料理　*2* 中国料理
3 日本料理　*4* イタリア料理

No. 12 正解 4

A: Excuse me. Has the nine-o'clock train to Boston already left?
B: Yes, ma'am. It left five minutes ago.
A: Wasn't it the last one today?
B: No, the last one leaves at ten.
Question: What time does the last train to Boston leave?

訳 A：すみません。ボストン行きの9時の電車はもう発車しましたか。
B：はい。5分前に出ました。
A：今日の終電ではないですか。
B：いいえ，最終電車は10時に出ますよ。
質問：ボストン行きの最終電車は何時に発車しますか。
▶ *1* 8時55分に。　*2* 9時に。
3 9時55分に。　*4* 10時に。

No. 13 正解 1

A: Have you moved to your new apartment, Cathy?
B: Yes. It's just a ten-minute walk from the office.
A: That's really nice. It takes me 40 minutes by car.
B: My last one was an hour away.
Question: How long does it take Cathy to get to work now?

訳 A：キャシー，新しいアパートに引っ越したのかい？
B：ええ。オフィスから歩いてたった10分のところなの。
A：それはすごくいいね。僕は車で40分かかるよ。
B：前のところは1時間の距離だったわ。
質問：今，キャシーは仕事場までどのくらいかかりますか。
▶ *1* 10分。　*2* 40分。
3 60分。　*4* 70分。

No. 14 正解 3

A: What's wrong, David?
B: I can't find my watch.
A: I saw it on the coffee table last night.
B: Really? I'll check.
Question: What is David's problem?

訳 A：デイビッド，どうしたの？
B：腕時計が見つからないんだよ。
A：昨夜，コーヒーテーブルの上で見たわよ。
B：本当に？　確かめてみるよ。
質問：デイビッドの問題は何ですか。
▶ *1* テーブルが見つからない。
2 コーヒーを飲まなかった。
3 腕時計をなくした。
4 昨夜，眠れなかった。

No. 15 正解 2

A: Dad, Mom just called. She's still working and won't be back before seven tonight.
B: Let's make dinner, then.
A: OK. What shall we make?
B: Beef steak and salad. Sound good?
Question: What are they going to do?

訳 A：お父さん，お母さんが電話してきたよ。まだ仕事中で，今夜は7時前には帰れないだろうって。
B：じゃあ，一緒に夕食を作ろう。
A：わかった。何を作ろうか？
B：ビーフステーキとサラダ。いいかい？
質問：彼らは何をしようとしていますか。
▶ *1* レストランへ行く。　*2* 夕食を作る。
3 ピザを注文する。　*4* 母親を待つ。

No. 16 正解 3

A: What do you want to do after college, Fred?
B: I want to teach English to foreign students.
A: Interesting. I want to be a dentist.
B: That's really good, Martha.
Question: What does Fred want to be in the future?

訳 A：フレッド，大学卒業後は何をしたい？
B：外国の生徒たちに英語を教えたいと思っているよ。
A：おもしろいわね。私は歯科医になりたいわ。
B：すごくいいね，マーサ。
質問：フレッドは将来何になりたいと思っていますか。
▶ *1* 歯科医。　*2* 看護師。
3 教師。　*4* ツアーガイド。

No. 17 正解 **3**

A: Why don't we study together today, Ann?

B: I'd like to, Charles, but I have to help my grandmother today.

A: How about tomorrow?

B: That will be fine.

Question: What is Ann going to do today?

訳 A：アン，今日一緒に勉強しようよ。

B：そうしたいんだけどね，チャールズ，今日は祖母を手伝わないといけないの。

A：明日はどう？

B：大丈夫よ。

質問：アンは今日，何をする予定ですか。

▶ *1* チャールズと勉強する。
2 自宅に友達を招待する。
3 祖母を手伝う。
4 家族と出かける。

No. 18 正解 **4**

A: I like your tie, Jeff. Is it new?

B: Yes, it is, Mary. I like this color so much.

A: Where did you find it?

B: My son bought it for me.

Question: Who bought Jeff's tie?

訳 A：いいネクタイね，ジェフ。新しいの？

B：そうだよ，メアリー。この色をとても気に入っているんだ。

A：どこで見つけたの？

B：息子が僕に買ってくれたんだよ。

質問：だれがジェフのネクタイを買いましたか。

▶ *1* メアリー。 *2* ジェフ。
3 ジェフの娘。 *4* ジェフの息子。

No. 19 正解 **4**

A: Have you ever been to Europe, Mark?

B: I've been to France and Spain. And I'm planning to visit Germany.

A: I've been to Italy twice and I'm going to visit it again next week.

B: Have a good time!

Question: Where will the woman go next week?

訳 A：マーク，これまでにヨーロッパに行ったことある？

B：フランスとスペインに行ったことがあるよ。そしてドイツを訪れる計画を立てているところだよ。

A：私はイタリアに2回行ったことがあって，来週，また訪れる予定なの。

B：楽しんできてね！

質問：女性は来週，どこに行きますか。

▶ *1* フランス。 *2* スペイン。
3 ドイツ。 *4* イタリア。

No. 20 正解 **2**

A: How much are these T-shirts?

B: They were twenty dollars last week, but now, only fifteen.

A: Then, I'll take these two.

B: That'll be thirty dollars, please.

Question: How much was a T-shirt last week?

訳 A：これらのTシャツはいくらですか。

B：先週は20ドルでしたが，今はたったの15ドルですよ。

A：それでは，この2着を買います。

B：30ドルになります。

質問：先週，Tシャツは1枚いくらでしたか。

▶ *1* 15ドル。 *2* 20ドル。 *3* 25ドル。 *4* 30ドル。

第3部

No. 21 **1**	***No. 22*** **1**	***No. 23*** **2**	***No. 24*** **3**
No. 25 **3**	***No. 26*** **3**	***No. 27*** **3**	***No. 28*** **2**
No. 29 **3**	***No. 30*** **4**		

No. 21 正解 **1**

Yuka is going to Okinawa next month. Her father is going, too, but her mother has to work. Yuka is going to buy some gifts for her mother and her friends.

Question: Who will go to Okinawa with Yuka?

訳 ユカは来月，沖縄へ行く予定です。父親も行きますが，母親は仕事があります。ユカは母親と自分の友達にプレゼントを買うつもりです。

質問：だれがユカと一緒に沖縄へ行きますか。

▶ *1* 父親。 *2* 母親。 *3* 兄［弟］。 *4* 友達。

No. 22 正解 **1**

Mike often loses his things. Last Friday, he lost his smartphone and found it the next day. This morning, he couldn't find his bike key, so he borrowed his sister's bike to go to school. He'll look for the key this afternoon.

Question: When did Mike lose his smartphone?

訳 マイクはよく物をなくします。この前の金曜日，スマートフォンをなくして，次の日に見つけました。今朝は自転車の鍵が見つからなかったので，学校へ行くのに姉［妹］の自転車を借りました。彼は今日の午後，鍵を探すつもりです。

質問：マイクはいつスマートフォンをなくしましたか。

▶ *1* この前の金曜日。 *2* この前の土曜日。 *3* 今朝。 *4* 今日の午後。

No. 23 正解 **2**

Harumi is studying Korean. She has classes on Wednesdays and Fridays. The lessons are for three hours. Every Friday after class, she goes to a Korean restaurant with her classmates.

Question: How many times a week does Harumi have Korean lessons?

訳 ハルミは韓国語を勉強しています。水曜日と金曜日に授業があります。授業は3時間です。毎週金曜日には授業のあと，クラスメートと一緒に韓国料理店へ行きます。

質問：ハルミは，1週間に何回，韓国語の授業がありますか。

▶ *1* 1回。 *2* 2回。 *3* 3回。 *4* 4回。

No. 24 正解 **3**

Last year, my volleyball team played 9 games. I played in 8 of them. We won 3 and lost 6. This year, we want to win at least 5 games.

Question: How many volleyball games did the boy play last year?

訳 昨年，僕のバレーボールチームは9試合しました。僕はそのうちの8試合でプレーしました。僕たちは3勝6敗でした。今年は，少なくとも5試合は勝ちたいです。

質問：男の子は昨年，バレーボールで何試合プレーしましたか。

▶ *1* 5。 *2* 6。 *3* 8。 *4* 9。

No. 25 正解 **3**

There is a beach near my house. I sometimes go there to walk my dog. This Sunday, some volunteers are going to collect garbage there. I'll join them.

Question: What will the girl do this Sunday?

訳 私の家の近くに浜辺があります。私はときどきそこで犬の散歩をします。今度の日曜日，ボランティアの人たちがそこでゴミを集めます。私は彼らに加わるつもりです。

質問：女の子は今度の日曜日に何をしますか。

▶ *1* 犬の散歩をする。 *2* 自分の家をそうじする。 *3* ゴミを集める。 *4* 海で泳ぐ。

No. 26 正解 **3**

Welcome to Jason's Clothing Store. Men's clothes are 10 percent off and women's clothes are 15 percent off. Kids' clothes are 20 percent off. And all hats are 30 percent off!

Question: What are 15 percent off?

訳 ジェイソン衣料品店へようこそ。男性服は10パーセント割引で，女性服は15パーセント割引です。子ども服は20パーセント割引。そして，ぼうしは全品30パーセント割引です。

質問：15パーセント割引なのは何ですか。

▶ *1* ぼうし。 *2* 男性服。 *3* 女性服。 *4* 子ども服。

No. 27 正解 **3**

Next week, my cousin is going to visit us. He's 19 now, but he'll be 20 when he comes. I'm 17 now, but will be 18 tomorrow. We're going to celebrate our birthdays together.

Question: How old is the cousin of the girl now?

訳 来週，いとこが私たちを訪ねてくる予定です。彼は今，19歳ですが，やって来るときには20歳になっています。私は今，17歳ですが，明日18歳になります。私たちは一緒に誕生日を祝う予定です。

質問：女の子のいとこは，今，何歳ですか。

▶ *1* 17歳。 *2* 18歳。 *3* 19歳。 *4* 20歳。

No. 28 正解 **2**

Some of my friends have dogs, but I have a cat. Her

name is Ruby and she's five years old. I play with her every day after school. She also likes to play with paper bags.

Question: What is the boy talking about?

訳 友達の何人かは犬を飼っていますが，僕は猫を飼っています。彼女の名前はルビーで，5歳です。僕は毎日放課後に彼女と遊びます。彼女は紙袋で遊ぶのも好きです。

質問：男の子は何について話していますか。

▶ ***1*** 友達の犬。　***2*** ペット。
3 学校。　***4*** 紙袋。

No. 29 正解 3

During our four-day trip to Kyoto, the weather was terrible. On Monday and Tuesday, it rained a lot. On Wednesday, it was cloudy and windy. On our last day, it even snowed.

Question: How was the weather on Tuesday?

訳 京都への4日間の旅行の間，天気はひどいものでした。月曜日と火曜日は，雨がたくさん降りました。水曜日には，くもって風が強かったです。最後の日には，雪さえも降りました。

質問：火曜日の天気はどうでしたか。

▶ ***1*** 晴れ。　***2*** くもり。
3 雨。　***4*** 雪。

No. 30 正解 4

There'll be a history test tomorrow. I need to study hard for it. But I'm going to be so busy today that there'll be very little time for that. I'm so worried.

Question: What's the boy's problem?

訳 明日，歴史の試験があります。僕はそれを必死に勉強する必要があります。でも，今日はとても忙しくて，そのための時間がほんの少ししかなさそうなのです。すごく心配です。

質問：男の子の問題は何ですか。

▶ ***1*** 数学が得意ではない。
2 明日，忙しくなる。
3 病気で寝ている。
4 勉強する時間がほとんどない。

二次試験（面接） 練習問題

問題カードの日本語訳

図書館

日本の多くの市や町には図書館があります。人々はそこで，多様な種類の本を読んだり借りたりできるので，図書館は訪れるのに人気の場所です。いくつかの図書館では，ボランティアが子どもにおもしろい物語を読んでくれます。

質問の日本語訳

No. 1 文章を見てください。人々は図書館で何ができますか。

No. 2 イラストを見てください。何人の少年がメガネをかけていますか。

No. 3 男性を見てください。彼は何を見ていますか。

No. 4 ふだんどうやって学校に行きますか。

No. 5 音楽を聴くことは好きですか。

はい。と答えた場合 → もっと詳しく話してください。

いいえ。と答えた場合 → ひまな時間に何をするのが好きですか。

解答例

No.1 They can read or borrow many different kinds of books.

No.2 Two boys are wearing glasses.

No.3 He is looking at the clock.

No.4 I walk to school.

No.5 Yes. → I like to listen to rock music.

No. → I like to watch TV.

解答例の日本語訳

▶ No. 1 多様な種類の本を読んだり借りたりできます。

No. 2 2人の少年がメガネをかけています。

No. 3 彼は(掛け)時計を見ています。

No. 4 私は歩いて学校に行きます。

No. 5 はい。 → 私はロック音楽を聴くのが好きです。

いいえ。→ 私はテレビを見るのが好きです。

切り取り線

記入上の注意（記述形式）
・指示事項を守り，文字は，はっきりわかりやすく書いてください。
・太枠に囲まれた部分のみが採点の対象です。

4 ライティング解答欄 （Eメール）

5

10

15

記入上の注意（記述形式）

・指示事項を守り，文字は，はっきりわかりやすく書いてください。

・太枠に囲まれた部分のみが採点の対象です。

切り取り線

5 ライティング解答欄 （英作文）

5

10

15

模擬試験 解答用紙

注意事項

①解答にはHBの黒鉛筆（シャープペンシルも可）を使用し，解答を訂正する場合には消しゴムで完全に消してください。

②解答用紙は絶対に汚したり折り曲げたり，所定以外のところへの記入はしないでください。

③マーク例

良い例	悪い例
●	⊙ ⊗ ◓

これ以下の濃さのマークは読めません。

解答欄					
問題番号		1	2	3	4
1	(1)	①	②	③	④
	(2)	①	②	③	④
	(3)	①	②	③	④
	(4)	①	②	③	④
	(5)	①	②	③	④
	(6)	①	②	③	④
	(7)	①	②	③	④
	(8)	①	②	③	④
	(9)	①	②	③	④
	(10)	①	②	③	④
	(11)	①	②	③	④
	(12)	①	②	③	④
	(13)	①	②	③	④
	(14)	①	②	③	④
	(15)	①	②	③	④

解答欄					
問題番号		1	2	3	4
2	(16)	①	②	③	④
	(17)	①	②	③	④
	(18)	①	②	③	④
	(19)	①	②	③	④
	(20)	①	②	③	④
3	(21)	①	②	③	④
	(22)	①	②	③	④
	(23)	①	②	③	④
	(24)	①	②	③	④
	(25)	①	②	③	④
	(26)	①	②	③	④
	(27)	①	②	③	④
	(28)	①	②	③	④
	(29)	①	②	③	④
	(30)	①	②	③	④

リスニング解答欄					
問題番号		1	2	3	4
第1部	No.1	①	②	③	
	No.2	①	②	③	
	No.3	①	②	③	
	No.4	①	②	③	
	No.5	①	②	③	
	No.6	①	②	③	
	No.7	①	②	③	
	No.8	①	②	③	
	No.9	①	②	③	
	No.10	①	②	③	

リスニング解答欄					
問題番号		1	2	3	4
第2部	No.11	①	②	③	④
	No.12	①	②	③	④
	No.13	①	②	③	④
	No.14	①	②	③	④
	No.15	①	②	③	④
	No.16	①	②	③	④
	No.17	①	②	③	④
	No.18	①	②	③	④
	No.19	①	②	③	④
	No.20	①	②	③	④

リスニング解答欄					
問題番号		1	2	3	4
第3部	No.21	①	②	③	④
	No.22	①	②	③	④
	No.23	①	②	③	④
	No.24	①	②	③	④
	No.25	①	②	③	④
	No.26	①	②	③	④
	No.27	①	②	③	④
	No.28	①	②	③	④
	No.29	①	②	③	④
	No.30	①	②	③	④

切り取り線